Global Finance and the Macroeconomy

Also by A.J. Makin

INTERNATIONAL CAPITAL MOBILITY AND EXTERNAL ACCOUNT DETERMINATION

OPEN ECONOMY MACROECONOMICS

Global Finance and the Macroeconomy

A.J. Makin
Reader in Economics
University of Queensland
Brisbane, Australia

First published in hardcover 2000

First published in paperback 2003 by
PALGRAVE MACMILLAN
Houndmills, Basingstoke, Hampshire RG21 6XS and
175 Fifth Avenue, New York, N. Y. 10010
Companies and representatives throughout the world

PALGRAVE MACMILLAN is the global academic imprint of the Palgrave Macmillan division of St. Martin's Press, LLC and of Palgrave Macmillan Ltd. Macmillan® is a registered trademark in the United States, United Kingdom and other countries. Palgrave is a registered trademark in the European Union and other countries.

ISBN 0–333–73698–2 hardback *(outside North America)*
ISBN 0–312–23128–8 hardback *(in North America)*
ISBN 1–4039–1893–7 paperback *(worldwide)*

This book is printed on paper suitable for recycling and made from fully managed and sustained forest sources.

A catalogue record for this book is available from the British Library.

Library of Congress Cataloging-in Publication Data
Makin, A.J.
    Global finance and the macroeconomy / A.J. Makin.
        p. cm.
    Includes bibliographical references and index.
    ISBN 1-4039-1893-7 (pbk.)
        1. International finance. 2. Macroeconomics. I. Title.

HG3881.M295 2003
332'.042--dc22
                                                2003053629

10   9   8   7   6   5   4   3   2   1
12   11   10   09   08   07   06   05   04   03

Printed and bound in Great Britain by
Antony Rowe Ltd, Chippenham and Eastbourne

Contents

List of Tables

List of Figures

xii *List of Figures*

Preface and Acknowledgements

International finance and open economy macroeconomics have grown strongly as sub-fields of economics over recent years, reflecting the rapid globalisation of markets for goods, services and assets and the need to understand its economy-wide implications. Accordingly, it is no longer sensible to interpret economic and financial behaviour for any country or region without regard to its international investment and trade flows which, ultimately, affect the welfare of all consumers and producers of goods and services.

The purpose of this book is to provide a thorough exposition of theoretical models in this area, also known as international monetary economics. These models, founded on solid international macroeconomic accounting foundations, link global capital flows and the main financial and real economy-wide variables, including exchange rates, interest rates, national output, national expenditure, exports, imports, the current account, foreign debt, money supplies and inflation.

A key feature of the analysis is its heavy reliance on graphical techniques to reinterpret ever important international monetary issues, such as the significance of external deficits, international capital mobility, interest differentials, capital flight and how monetary and fiscal policies operate in open economies.

Of necessity, this work draws in part on my earlier book, *International Capital Mobility and External Account Determination*, one of the first books to expound and extend capital-theoretic approaches to the open economy, including the now popular intertemporal model. However, it earns its status as a new book through inclusion of substantial new material on a wider range of related themes, such as financial globalisation, the international flow of funds, international parity relations, exchange rate behaviour, monetary and fiscal policy and financial crises in emerging economies.

Finally, thanks are due to those individuals most closely involved in the production process, especially to Amy Lindley, Robyn McDonald and Brenda Marshall of The University of Queensland, and to Amanda Watkins, Alison Howson, Keith Povey and the team at the publishers.

TONY MAKIN

1
Evolution of the International Financial System

The collapse of the Bretton Woods system of fixed exchange rates in the early 1970s marked the last major turning point in the evolution of global finance, ushering in the generalised 'non-system' of exchange rate arrangements that survives today. However, at least as important in the development of international financial relations since then has been the enormous growth in the volume of international capital flows. In large part, this growth is attributable to the dismantling of the panoply of exchange controls introduced during the Bretton Woods era to facilitate exchange rate management by central banks under the auspices of the International Monetary Fund (IMF).

Increased capital flows have been directed toward both advanced and developing economies alike. Major users of international funds include Australia, Britain, Canada, New Zealand and the United States, as well as the so-called 'emerging economies'. The emerging economies are a culturally and geographically diverse group of international borrower countries whose membership presently includes Argentina, Brazil, Chile, Colombia, Hungary, the Czech Republic, India, Indonesia, Israel, Malaysia, Korea, Mexico, Pakistan, Peru, the Philippines, South Africa, Thailand, Turkey and Venezuela.

The range of deregulatory initiatives affecting domestic and international financial transactions over recent decades include the abolition of capital and interest rate controls and the entry of foreign financial institutions to domestic markets. These measures, combined with technological progress in telecommunications, greatly reduced transactions costs and widespread financial innovation have broken down barriers separating economies' financial markets.

The domestic financial markets of many economies have therefore been increasingly internationalised in the wake of liberalising policy initiatives implemented by governments around the world. Financial market liberalisation in many advanced economies was virtually complete by the late 1980s. With the removal of previously stringent regulations over domestic and international financial transactions, institutional barriers impeding the movement of financial capital between many regions of the world have now largely disappeared. Accompanying the domestic deregulatory changes were tighter prudential arrangements in advanced economies aimed at strengthening the capitalisation of banks and hence the stability of domestic financial systems. Such accompanying arrangements have been lacking in many emerging economies however and this has been a fundamental reason for recurrent financial crises in these economies, as subsequently discussed in this book.

Another way of defining the phenomenon of financial globalisation is to say that domestic capital markets have become far more internationally integrated, such a process being the financial counterpart to the worldwide rise in cross-border trade in goods and services. Assisted by significant improvements in computer technology and falling transactions costs, this has resulted in record growth in international money flows.

1.1   The scale of international financial flows

The global liberalisation of financial markets has facilitated a phenomenal rise in the movement of funds across country borders. Aided by major advances in information technology and reduced computing and communications costs, this international capital market integration has greatly improved access to the pool of global saving for advanced and emerging economies. This has given rise to substantially increased capital mobility, with national saving and investment rates no longer as closely correlated as in earlier decades.

The associated current account imbalances at times have attracted the attention of policy-makers, prompting attempts to narrow them. Yet, to presume that current accounts should be approximately balanced implies that individual economies should be neither exporters nor importers of capital. Is this economically justifiable? Indeed, could greater capital outflows matching higher current account surpluses have benefited some countries, at the same time as greater capital inflows matching current account deficits benefited others? Answers to theoretical questions like these are provided in later chapters.

For many economies, current account imbalances as a proportion of GDP have been substantially higher in recent decades compared with, for instance, imbalances experienced in earlier decades when prohibitive exchange controls were in place. Nonetheless, international funds may be no more mobile across borders today than in the relatively frictionless international environment of the late nineteenth century and the early decades of this century. For example, the flow of capital from the United Kingdom persistently averaged over 5 per cent of GDP between 1870 and 1913, while the flow of capital into Canada reached a peak of 13 per cent of GDP between 1910 and 1913.[1]

International money market activity of this order and the lightning speed at which funds can now quit countries has also prompted many commentators to question its worth and, in light of heightened vulnerability to foreign investor sentiment, to emphasise its perceived dangers. In particular, strong objections to the ever-increasing trend of financial globalisation have been raised on the grounds that the governments of the economies most affected have ceded their economic sovereignty to international investors.

Accordingly, it is said that the priorities and policy choices facing national governments can no longer be considered and implemented without first taking possible foreign investor reactions into account. Yet it can be shown that financial globalisation actually tends to improve, rather than worsen, a nation's overall economic welfare and that having an internationally integrated economy provides a safeguard against irresponsible growth limiting and inflationary policies.

Though exchange controls have been progressively dismantled since the early 1970s, their removal in emerging economies quickly accelerated throughout the 1980s and 1990s according to an index of capital controls devised by the International Monetary Fund.[2] Figure 1.1 shows where capital flows have recently been directed. At the same time, institutional investors in advanced economies increasingly became more aware of opportunities to diversify portfolios and more internationalised banks were readier to lend in emerging markets. Table 1.1 reveals the nature and scale of capital flows to emerging markets over recent decades. By the end of the century, emerging economies were absorbing over 40 per cent of global foreign direct investment compared with 15 per cent in 1990, and received 30 per

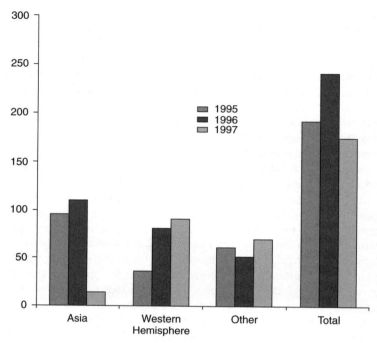

Figure 1.1   Capital inflows by region (US$ billion)

cent of global portfolio equity flows as against around 2 per cent in the early 1990s.

When countries are net borrowers of funds from the rest of the world they experience current account deficits, the size of which also approximately measure net capital inflow from external sources. The

Table 1.1   Capital flows to emerging markets annual averages (US$ billion)

	1977–82	1983–89	1990–94	1995	1996	1997
All emerging markets						
Total net capital inflows	30.5	8.8	120.8	192.0	240.8	173.7
Net foreign direct investment	11.2	13.3	46.2	96.0	114.9	138.2
Net portfolio investment	–10.5	6.5	61.1	23.5	49.7	42.9
Other[a]	29.8	–11.0	13.5	72.5	76.2	–7.3

[a]Includes bank lending, 1977–89 figures exclude economies in transition and some Middle Eastern emerging markets.
Sources: IMF 1995, p. 33; IMF 1998, p. 13.

relative sizes of the current account balances of significant net borrower and lender economies over recent years are shown in Table 1.2.

Over recent decades, funds have mostly flowed across country borders as bank lending or to acquire debt instruments, although considerable foreign equity investment has also occurred, especially after the privatisation of state enterprises in many economies. The estimated outstanding amount of international debt securities reached over $US 3 trillion by the late 1990s, whereas international bank loans have also more than tripled over the past decade. Meanwhile, the turnover on the global foreign exchange market, which facilitates the international borrowing and lending process, presently exceeds an average $US 2 trillion in value every day, as indicated in Table 1.3. This volume of foreign exchange trading today is a large multiple of its value at the end of the 1980s.

1.2   A short history of global finance

The macroeconomic significance of international financial flows and external payments imbalances critically depends on prevailing exchange rate arrangements, as well as the extent of official restrictions in the form of capital controls. To put the existing global financial system in historical context, it is necessary to consider the evolution of the international monetary and financial system. The development of the international financial order from its beginnings to the present day is summarised in Table 1.4.

The gold standard is usually dated from the later part of the nineteenth century when the main industrial economies of Europe and North America defined their currencies in terms of gold, though some of these countries had used gold for international settlements from much earlier times.

During the First World War, 1914–18, the gold standard was suspended and afterwards the currencies of Britain, France and many other nations floated quite freely until returning to the old rules from the mid-1920s. From the early 1930s, many countries again abandoned gold and through to the end of the Second World War the international monetary system was characterised by economic nationalism, competitive devaluations and the proliferation of trade barriers and capital controls.[3]

In light of the 1930s experience, delegates from 44 nations met at Bretton Woods, New Hampshire, to produce the Articles of Agreement

Table 1.2   Current account balances: select economies (per cent of GDP)

	1997	1998	1999	2000
Advanced economies				
United States	–1.9	–2.7	–3.5	–3.3
Japan	2.2	3.2	3.6	3.4
Germany	–0.2	–0.4	–0.1	–
France	2.8	2.7	2.8	3.0
Italy	3.0	2.3	2.3	2.3
United Kingdom	0.6	–0.8	–1.2	–1.4
Canada	–1.5	–2.1	–1.6	–1.1
Australia	–3.1	–5.0	–5.4	–5.0
Austria	–2.2	–2.0	–1.5	–1.3
Belgium-Luxembourg	5.6	5.3	5.3	5.4
Denmark	0.5	–1.4	–0.8	–0.2
Finland	5.5	5.1	5.2	4.9
Greece	–2.6	–2.6	–2.5	–2.6
Hong Kong SAR	–3.2	0.6	1.2	1.2
Ireland	2.8	1.9	1.9	1.8
Israel	–3.3	–3.0	–2.6	–2.2
Korea	–1.8	13.1	7.1	4.1
Netherlands	6.1	5.6	5.4	5.8
New Zealand	–7.1	–6.0	–6.7	–5.8
Norway	5.2	–0.8	1.4	2.9
Portugal	–2.2	–4.1	–3.7	–3.7
Singapore	15.8	20.9	18.0	17.7
Spain	0.5	–0.2	–0.8	–0.8
Sweden	2.9	2.1	1.9	1.7
Switzerland	8.9	9.1	9.3	9.4
Taiwan Province of China	2.7	1.3	2.0	2.0
Memorandum: Euro area	1.7	1.4	1.5	1.6
Developing countries				
Algeria	7.2	–2.0	–3.6	–0.6
Argentina	–3.7	–4.4	–4.3	–4.3
Brazil	–4.1	–4.5	–3.0	–2.6
Cameroon	–1.3	–2.5	–4.4	–4.4
Chile	–5.3	–6.3	–5.0	–4.9
China	3.3	2.4	1.7	1.1
Côte d'Ivoire	–4.5	–4.9	–2.9	–2.5
Egypt	0.2	–3.0	–3.9	–3.8
India	–1.4	–1.7	–1.9	–2.2
Indonesia	–3.0	3.4	2.7	1.5
Malaysia	–5.1	15.7	9.6	5.0
Mexico	–1.9	–3.7	–2.0	–2.2
Nigeria	4.8	–8.4	–11.5	–5.8

Table 1.2   (continued)

	1997	1998	1999	2000
Pakistan	−5.8	−2.9	−2.8	−2.6
Philippines	−5.2	2.0	2.5	1.5
Saudi Arabia	0.2	−10.4	−8.2	−6.9
South Africa	−1.5	−2.1	−1.4	−1.6
Thailand	−1.9	12.2	8.8	5.5
Turkey	−1.4	1.4	1.0	0.1
Uganda	−0.9	−2.1	−3.6	−2.6
Countries in transition				
Czech Republic	−6.1	−1.8	−2.0	−1.7
Estonia	−13.0	−8.9	−7.1	−7.9
Hungary	−2.2	−4.1	−4.9	−4.7
Latvia	−4.8	−8.4	−7.3	−6.0
Lithuania	−10.2	−12.1	−12.8	−11.8
Poland	−3.1	−4.5	−5.6	−4.3
Russia	−1.3	0.3	8.4	8.2
Slovak Republic	−10.6	−10.3	−4.5	−3.4
Ukraine	−2.7	−1.5	−2.5	−2.2

Source: International Monetary Fund, *World Economic Outlook*, May 1999, p. 42.

of the International Monetary Fund in 1944. This new set of rules (the Bretton Woods system) included the maintenance of stable exchange rates, with the value of the United States dollar in terms of gold playing a pivotal role. The system broke down from the early 1970s, however, when the gold value of the United States dollar could no longer be sustained. Thereafter, the exchange rates of leading industrial nations were essentially determined in foreign exchange markets.

Official attitudes to controlling international capital flows have changed dramatically since the Second World War. While the IMF articles of agreement actually sanctioned exchange controls as a supplement to exchange rate management, in contrast, the Code of

Table 1.3 Foreign exchange market turnover ($US trillion)

1992	1998
0.6	2.0

Source: International Monetary Fund (1999a), p. 31.

Table 1.4   A chronology of international monetary arrangements

Late 1800s	Gold standard
1914–18	World War I
1919–25	Fluctuating exchange rates
1925–31	Restored gold standard
1931–40	Managed exchange rates, disorder
1940–45	World War II
1945–71	Bretton Woods era
Early 1970s–today	Exchange rate 'non-system'; high capital mobility

Liberalisation of Capital Movements, first drafted by the Organisation for Economic Cooperation and Development (OECD) in the 1960s, proposed that international capital movements be progressively freed. With the breakdown of the Bretton Woods system of exchange rate management, and in accordance with the OECD Code, financial markets were progressively liberalised with implications for capital flows, the effectiveness of monetary and fiscal policy and nations' external accounts. The presumption that international merchandise trade was to be encouraged after the war through a supranational institution like the General Agreement on Tariffs and Trade did not extend beyond trade in goods to include freer international trade in saving or financial services.

Indeed, there was widespread antipathy toward free international capital movements at the time, as reflected for instance in a comment by John Maynard Keynes (1933), an architect of the Bretton Woods monetary system, that

> Ideas, knowledge, science, hospitality, travel – these are the things which should of their nature be international. But let goods be homespun whenever it is reasonable and conveniently possible, and above all else let finance be primarily national.

Keynes also declared that 'nothing is more certain than that the movement of capital funds must be regulated'. Interestingly, the IMF now actively promotes capital account liberalisation for member economies, in contrast to its Bretton Woods-era policy of sanctioning the earlier wideranging measures that restricted international capital flows.

Both domestic and international financial transactions had been tightly controlled for much of the postwar era. For instance, at the domestic level there were often quantitative limits on bank lending, and deposit and lending rates were sometimes directly controlled by central banks. A range of capital controls also impeded international financial flows including prohibitions on capital outflows and embargoes on short-term inflows. With the removal of such restrictions from the 1970s onwards, external borrowing and lending began to rise sharply. Some deregulatory measures had direct implications for both domestic and international financial transactions. For example, the licensing of foreign banks in domestic markets increased competitive pressures generally at the same time as it facilitated domestic firms' access to new sources of foreign saving.

The volume of both international capital inflows and outflows increased in the new deregulated environment of the final quarter of the century, and the single most significant deregulatory measure which contributed to this was the abolition of exchange controls over the international movement of financial flows. There was also greatly increased fundraising through the Eurodollar markets which was not, of itself, a product of deregulatory measures adopted by industrial nations at home, but a consequence of institutional developments outside the sphere of traditional financial markets.

Two fundamental causes have internationalised production and finance – improvements in technology and the liberalisation of markets for goods, services and saving. Technological advances in electronics have greatly reduced the costs of communication and computing, conquering the natural barriers of time and distance. The cost of a three-minute telephone call between Sydney and London, for instance is, at less than $5, hundredths of what the cost of such a call would have been back in 1930. Since that time, the invention of computing and new ways of instantly transmitting information around the world in print form, such as by facsimile, email and the internet have reconstructed international communications. More generally, computers have revolutionised the processing and dissemination of information, its use greatly encouraged by the fact that since the mid-1970s the cost of computer processing has been falling by an average of 30 per cent per year in real terms.

Through the World Trade Organisation (WTO), and its predecessor body the General Agreement on Tariffs and Trade (GATT), many governments around the world have been actively promoting freer international trade in goods and services over recent decades, though not without serious disagreement along the way. The WTO itself has a mandate to continue reducing tariffs and non-tariff barriers in accordance with the tenets of multilateral cooperation. Large trading groups, such as the North American Free Trade Agreement (NAFTA), the European Union and the Asia-Pacific Economic Cooperation forum (APEC) have also been created for the very purpose of encouraging greater cross-border trade and investment flows by dismantling policy-initiated impediments to trade such as import tariffs.

The phenomenon of globalisation is not, however, an economic phenomenon that first began in, or is exclusive to, the late twentieth century. The world economy previously experienced an era of globalisation similar in many respects to the present one that began in the second half of the last century, but which was ended by the First World War. This first era of globalisation coincided with the gold standard system that governed all international economic transactions during which many economies were increasingly internationalised by large trade and investment flows, encouraged by the emergence of additional markets in the New World.

Throughout this particular phase of world development there were also substantial movements of people, emigrating mainly from Britain and Europe to colonies and former colonies in North America, South America, Africa and Australasia. In common with the current era of globalisation, the earlier era was also spurred by major breakthroughs in technology that greatly improved transport and communications, such as the telegraph, railways and steamships.

At the beginning of this century, international capital flows between some nations, such as Britain, Australia and Canada, as reflected in current account imbalances, actually exceeded levels of today when measured relative to national production. The share of exports in world output for instance, reached a peak in 1913 that was not surpassed again until 1970. Moreover, in the first globalisation era, migration rates and international labour mobility were proportionately higher than they are today. Yet, the earlier globalisation era was actually less global in its geographical reach than in the present era because today much larger parts of the world including throughout Asia, Latin America and Eastern Europe are affected than before.

Following the First World War, international goods markets generally *disintegrated* during the 1920s and this reversal of the rise of globalisation continued through the 1930s and 1940s as a result of escalating tariffs on internationally traded goods, unstable exchange rates, the Great Depression and the Second World War. Near the end of that war, a new international institution, the International Monetary Fund (IMF) was established to oversee the Bretton Woods system that lasted from 1945 to the early 1970s. The General Agreement on Tariffs and Trade (GATT) was also founded at this time for the purpose of scaling back tariffs and other protective measures that had restricted growth in international trade.

Under the Bretton Woods system which aimed to restore the exchange rate stability of the gold standard era, international capital flows were heavily controlled in order to assist central banks maintain exchange rates at predetermined levels. A major reason why nations agreed to fix exchange rates was that this was seen as a way of minimising exchange rate uncertainty that was thought to deter international trade flows.[4] The system eventually collapsed however because the fixed exchange rates it promoted could not be sustained in a global financial environment where international capital flows were continually growing, at times circumventing official investment barriers erected by national governments. The irony, was that this strong growth in international capital flows was in part attributable to a reemergence of increased volumes of exports and imports of goods and services that often had to be financed.

So, in a sense, the Bretton Woods system that had been designed to facilitate globalisation as it applied to increasing trade in goods and services, itself became a victim of globalisation as it applied to increased flows of international finance. Yet, despite the earlier views of the architects of the Bretton Woods system, the worldwide fluctuations in exchange rates that have occurred since the 1970s under the present 'non-system' of international monetary arrangements have not in fact stymied the growth of international trade. On the contrary, trade volumes have continued to rise thanks to the development of sophisticated measures of exchange rate risk management.

1.3 Financial globalisation: benefits and risks

These days few economists dispute the proposition that free trade in goods and services enhances overall economic welfare. By enabling greater international division of labour and more effective allocation of resources, including saving and finance, globalisation allows economies to reap rewards from specialisation in production. It also allows consumers in those economies to enjoy a wider range of product choice at the cheapest price.[5]

This is not to deny that there are losers from the process of liberalising trade, the worst affected being the owners and employees of previously highly protected industries who find it difficult to compete with more efficient foreign producers. Yet while there is apparent widespread agreement amongst economists and policy-makers about the longer term benefits of free trade in goods and services, there is less recognition of the benefits of free investment. For instance, many commentators neglect that as a result of foreign investment, many economies have been able to invest more domestically, and hence grow faster than otherwise, while generating higher yields for international investors.

In theory, greater international capital market integration and increased international borrowing and lending confers economy-wide benefits on borrower and lender economies alike. The greater availability of foreign funds to resident firms and households bestows clear-cut microeconomic and macroeconomic benefits to the extent that such funds make additional domestic economic activity possible. In this way, capital inflows directed toward financing extra domestic investment improve the growth prospects and hence long-term living standards of recipient countries. In other words, if foreign funds help fund more investment, this then allows more physical output to be produced, which in turn benefits residents through higher national income.

On this basis, the process of international capital market integration and the associated rise in international capital mobility has been, in theory, a welcome development. A corollary is that changes in domestic saving and investment rates are less well-correlated than when national capital markets were segmented and that, relatedly, domestic and foreign interest rates are more closely aligned after allowing for expected exchange rate movements and country risk. Meanwhile, foreign lenders have also benefited from the process to the extent they have been able to earn higher returns than elsewhere. Moreover, because movements in national stockmarket prices are rarely fully synchronised with stockmarket prices in major lending countries, it is possible for investors to reduce the overall volatility of their portfolios through international portfolio diversification. In general, therefore, foreign investment in any form confers income gains on both residents and non-residents alike because there are mutual gains to be reaped from international trade in financial assets.

International capital market integration has also changed the way domestic fiscal and monetary policies were thought to influence economic behaviour. Now with globally integrated financial markets, foreign investors are able to pass judgement quickly on governments' economic policies. If such policies in any particular economy are perceived as unsound, international finance is suddenly withdrawn, with immediate implications for its exchange rate, interest rates, expenditure and production.

The vulnerability of economies to international capital movements that many critics of financial globalisation find unacceptable quite simply arises from the fact that foreigners take a considerable risk when investing abroad. This risk is mainly due to factors such as uncertainty about future exchange rate movements, the possibility of default and unexpectedly poor returns. Hence, it is always in foreign investors' interests to carefully appraise an economy's fundamentals and economic policy settings before committing their money to economic ventures which lie outside their more familiar domain. If changes in an economy's policies increase the riskiness of present or potential investment, then foreigners can simply express their disapproval by investing elsewhere, in effect by voting with their funds.

Although greatly improved access to international capital has contributed to high economic growth rates of emerging economies over recent decades by enabling higher investment and production, international capital flow reversals have also precipitated some severe financial crises in emerging economies, which have caused recession, social hardship and political unrest. The adverse consequences of these financial crises have elicited renewed calls for the reimposition of Bretton Woods-style capital controls. As argued in the conclusion of this book, however, strengthening local financial systems is a better crisis prevention measure than restricting capital flows or imposing supranational taxes.

Another distinguishing feature of the latest era of globalisation is the role and prevalence of the multinational company, many of which have turnovers in excess of the national incomes of individual economies. Most of these multinationals are headquartered in the United States, Western Europe or Japan. Governments of different political persuasions around the world, today compete to attract foreign investment of this type, sometimes using specific tax concessions and subsidies for this purpose on the grounds that it is generally thought to allow the transfer of technology with positive implications for long-run economic growth.

1.4   Plan of this book

With the ever-increasing integration of most economies in the world, the phenomena of capital flows, interest rate and exchange rate fluctuations, external account imbalances, foreign debt levels and economic growth are as important to understand as ever before. Accordingly, it is no longer meaningful to interpret economic and financial behaviour for any nation or region without regard to its international trade and investment flows. Moreover, international financial flows have a significant impact on the operation and effectiveness of economies' monetary and fiscal policies for given exchange rate arrangements in the short run and on their productive capacity in the long run.

The aim of this book is to thoroughly analyse the relationship between international investment flows and macroeconomic activity by examining the linkages between capital flows, domestic and foreign interest rates, exchange rates, national output, employment, expenditure, the current account and national price levels. To achieve its objective, the book presents a suite of largely compatible approaches for understanding the key issues in international finance and open economy macroeconomics. It outlines new ways of analysing perennially important international economic issues, such as the significance of external deficits, capital mobility, interest rates and exchange rates and how monetary and fiscal policies operate via financial and real variables to influence the macroeconomy. The book is structured as follows.

Chapter 2 provides the external accounting and measurement foundations necessary for the subsequent theoretical and policy analysis. As background to the exposition of modern international monetary models, Chapter 3 critically surveys early approaches to external adjustment, including the classical, elasticities, absorption and monetary models. This chapter highlights the contributions of these models, while also drawing attention to their limitations.

Chapter 4 exposits the intertemporal model of the open economy. This contemporary approach demonstrates the macroeconomic significance of capital mobility, external imbalances and the economy-wide welfare gains that accrue from international trade in saving. The intertemporal model of Chapter 4 also provides the foundations of the loanable funds approach. The loanable funds approach is extended in Chapter 5 and used to reinterpret the standard interest rate parity conditions of international finance. This chapter also brings the exchange rate to the forefront, showing how it behaves in an alternative intertemporal framework in the presence of macroeconomic shocks and under conditions where domestic and foreign investors' expectations are asymmetric.

Chapter 6 addresses the transmission of macroeconomic policy in open economies as proposed by the Keynesian inspired Mundell–Fleming model. This chapter explains how international macroeconomic variables behave in response to expenditure and monetary shocks, yet also provides an extensive critique of the still popular Mundell–Fleming model, highlighting its deficiencies as a vehicle for understanding international macroeconomic policy. Chapter 7 presents an alternative international monetary framework for understanding macroeconomic policy that is consistent with open economy budget constraints and the conventional parity relationships of international finance. Unlike other international macroeconomic approaches, this new framework explicitly identifies how output, expenditure, the current account and the price level behave under circumstances where foreign investors immediately react to domestic policy changes.

Chapter 8 examines the longer-run role that international capital flows play in the economic growth process of open economies. It explicitly identifies foreign capital as a source of output growth and shows how various shocks affecting domestic capital accumulation can influence long-run macroeconomic performance. Chapter 9 concludes the book by analysing how and why economic and financial crises tend to occur in emerging economies that have attracted large-scale international financial flows. It assesses alternative economic policy responses to the economic and financial distress caused by international capital flow reversals to emerging economies. This chapter also reflects on the future course of financial globalisation.

2
Accounting and Measurement Issues

This chapter defines the international macroeconomic variables referred to later in this book and the accounting relationships which link them. A thorough understanding of these preliminaries is important since they form the basis for much of the subsequent theoretical and policy discussion.

In an open economy, resident households, firms and governments are perpetually linked through the prices and quantities of goods, services and financial assets they buy and sell from foreigners. Whenever funds are exchanged between a resident and non-resident entity, the transaction is recorded in the nation's external accounts as well as, but with opposite sign, in the corresponding accounts of the non-resident's country. Balance of payments accounting records a nation's international trade in goods, services and assets and is important because it indicates the size and direction of international financial flows. As a summary of all such transactions, the external accounts are a subset of the national accounts and hence are best considered in an international macroeconomic framework.

2.1 Open economy accounting relations

2.1.1 Absorption, income and the current account

In a closed economy, *ex post* the value of *gross domestic product* (Y) equals *gross national expenditure*. However, in an open economy, total spending by resident households and firms is the *absorption* of domestically produced goods and services (A), as well as goods and services produced abroad. The difference between residents' spending on domestically produced goods and total absorption is *imports* (M). *Exports* (X) on the other hand, represent foreign spending on domestic product and equal the difference between national product and residents' spending on locally produced goods and services. In sum, therefore, $Y = A + (X - M)$. Accordingly,

$$Y - A = X - M \tag{2.1}$$

If absorption exceeds output, the *trade balance* (T) is in deficit.

Another important distinction used subsequently is that between gross domestic product and *national income* (Y_n). The difference between these aggregates is due to *net income paid abroad* (y_a), the bulk of which is interest and dividends on existing *net external liabilities*, and *consumption of fixed capital* or depreciation allowances (d) such that $Y_n = Y - y_a - d$. Further, the national accounting term, *national disposable income* (Y_d), is national income less *net transfers paid abroad* (t). Therefore, $Y_d = Y_n - t$. The *current account balance* (CAB) is defined as $CAB = T + y_a + t$. The CAB recorded in the external accounts corresponds to the entry *net borrowing abroad* (B^*) recorded in the national accounts except that net borrowing abroad does not include *undistributed income* (u) accruing overseas.

The accounting relationships between the aggregates defined above, including gross domestic product, absorption, the trade balance, national income, national disposable income, the current account balance and net borrowing abroad are schematically depicted in Figure 2.1.

2.1.2   Saving, investment and the external accounts

It is now possible to introduce the intertemporal dimension of national accounting by recognising that *gross saving* (S) is the difference between *gross national product* (Y) and *consumption* (C) whereas *gross domestic investment* (I) is the difference between total absorption and consumption. Hence

$$(Y - C) - (A - C) = S - I = X - M \tag{2.2}$$

Therefore, when the trade balance is in deficit, not only must imports exceed exports, but gross investment must exceed gross domestic saving.

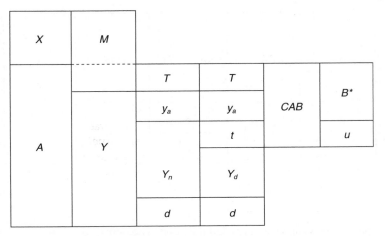

Figure 2.1 Absorption, income and the current account

Domestic saving (S_d) is defined as the difference between national disposable income (Y_d) and consumption. Net domestic investment I_d is the difference between gross investment and depreciation allowances. From the above definitions, it follows algebraically that

$$S_d - I_d = X - M - y_a - t = CAB \qquad (2.3)$$

Technically, consumption of fixed capital (d) is of little concern when focusing on the external imbalance as the saving-investment gap. It is immaterial whether gross or net measures are used to measure external imbalance because from equation (2.3)

$$CAB = S_d - I_d = (S - d) - (I - d) = S - I \qquad (2.4)$$

Whereas in a closed economy saving must always equal investment *ex post*, in an open economy the *CAB* provides a measure of the difference between these aggregates. When there is a current account deficit (*CAD*), the excess of net domestic investment over saving must be financed by foreign funds or *net capital inflow*, as measured by *net foreign investment* (*NFI*) or the *capital account surplus* (*KAS*). Hence an open economy can augment its *capital stock* (*K*) through the process of foreign investment. At the same time foreign investment increases the

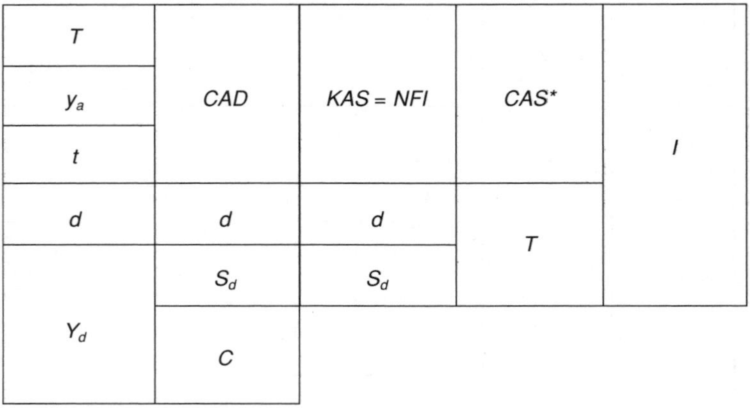

T				
y_a	CAD	KAS = NFI	CAS*	
t				I
d	d	d	T	
	S_d	S_d		
Y_d	C			

Figure 2.2 Saving, investment and the external accounts

domestic economy's stock of net external financial liabilities. There-fore, the larger is the rise in the nation's capital stock, given the level of domestic saving, the larger is the net capital inflow.

Through the use of foreign saving (S^*), as recorded by a capital account surplus, an economy's domestic investment can therefore be greater than otherwise, for without foreign capital inflow, the level of domestic investment can be constrained by the pool of domestic saving. When foreigners finance expansion of the domestic capital stock, the rise in net external liabilities or *net international investment position* is therefore matched by an increase in the nation's real assets, although the cost of borrowing from foreigners eventually and sometimes almost immediately appears in the current account as income paid overseas. Income paid overseas can therefore be perceived as the return to foreigners for allowing an economy to expand its capital stock. Figure 2.2 represents the relationships between foreign saving, domestic saving and investment, the *national capital account*, and the external accounts.

A nation's *NFI* must be matched by a corresponding current account surplus experienced by the rest of the world (CAS^*), and this must also equal the rest of the world's capital account deficit (KAD^*) against the home economy. Figure 2.3 depicts the accounting relationships between saving and investment at home and abroad and the international accounts.

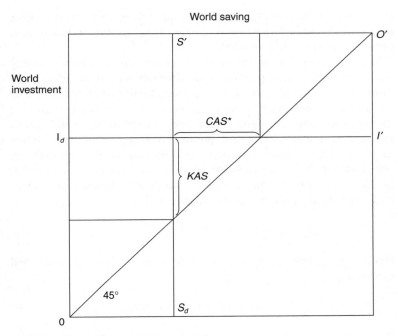

Figure 2.3 World saving and investment

Domestic saving (S_d) and net domestic investment (I_d) along with external saving (S) and net investment abroad (I) comprise world saving (S_W) and world investment (I_W). That is

$$I_w = I_d + I' = S_w = S_d + S' \qquad (2.5)$$

Current and capital account imbalances therefore reflect regions' saving and investment patterns. That is

$$I_d - S_d = NFI = CAD = KAS = S' - I' = CAS^* = KAD^* \qquad (2.6)$$

Only if domestic saving in each region fully finances domestic investment will the external accounts record a zero current or capital account balance. In the figure, this means external balance so defined includes all points on the 45° line. However, when saving is free to cross international borders, domestic capital formation can be higher for a nation with a *KAS* whereas abroad capital formation is less than otherwise to the extent of *CAS**.

The discussion has so far assumed an economy without a public sector. However, the public sector through its public enterprises produces output and through its spending, taxing and borrowing also contributes significantly to national absorption and the demand for saving in an open economy. Total public absorption (G) is the sum of public consumption (C_g) and public investment (I_g). The budget or public account imbalance provides a measure of the gap between public saving (S_g) – the difference between net tax revenue (T_g) and public consumption expenditure (C_g) and public investment expenditure (I_g). That is, the budget imbalance is

$$T_g - G = (T_g - C_g - I_g = S_g - I_g) \qquad (2.7)$$

Private and public saving add up to domestic saving (S_d) as defined earlier as

$$Y_d - C_p - C_g = S_d = (Y_d - T_g - C_p) + (T_g - C_g) = S_p + S_g \qquad (2.8)$$

Since the external account imbalance is the domestic saving-investment imbalance

$$NFI = KAS = CAD = (I_p - S_p) + (I_g - S_g) \qquad (2.9)$$

If the government's overall budget is balanced $(S_g = I_g)$, *NFI* is solely attributable to the private sector's investment-saving imbalance.

2.1.3   Valuation effects

In the foregoing discussion of the value of the balances in the external accounts, it was implicitly assumed that it was appropriate to measure external imbalances in domestic currency terms. However, there are valuation effects on international trade flows and on the servicing of foreign debt that arise due to movements in the economy exchange rate. To provide a hypothetical example of this phenomenon, focussing on the trade balance, assume imports were $200 million and exports $100 million, yielding a trade deficit of $100 million. After a 50 per cent depreciation, import and export prices may rise by up to the same percentage amount, so that the trade deficit could reach $150 million, other things the same. This valuation effect, sometimes referred to as a 'J-curve' effect, simply arises from the fact that following a currency depreciation, import values can be affected by more in domestic currency terms than export values if starting from a deficit position.

Such valuation effects suggest that a foreign currency measure of the imbalance may for some purposes provide a more meaningful measure of trends, particularly if the focus is the magnitude of capital flows viewed from a foreign perspective. This is also how column six of the real and financial flows matrix (Figure 2.4) actually presents net capital inflow. Moreover, if a reason for concern about a rising *CAD*, is its effect on the sentiment of foreign investors themselves, or if it is necessary to gauge the extent of foreign currency saving being exchanged for domestically created assets, it is more appropriate to present the external balance in foreign currency terms.

In principle, since every international transaction recorded in one economy's external accounts should be debited on another economy's, the sum of external balances for the world as a whole should be zero. In practice, however, the world's external account does not balance, but tends to show a persistent deficit. Reasons for this include measurement errors in the accounts other than valuation effects, related to factors such as under-recorded interest credits from abroad.

2.2   International financial flows and national wealth

2.2.1   Asset markets and the external accounts

It is now possible to introduce asset markets, financial instruments and the financial sector into a more general flow of funds framework. The stylised accounting matrix below (Figure 2.4) integrates the external accounts into the macroeconomy via its asset markets. This matrix will be referred to in subsequent chapters outlining the theoretical approaches to analysing the open economy.

The matrix includes firms, households, the government, financial intermediaries and the central bank as the main sectors of the economy and records their economic and financial transactions with the rest of the world. Hence, it adds financial intermediaries (commercial banks and other financial institutions) and the central bank as agents in the macroeconomy. There are seven markets in which all real economic

Market	(1) Households	(2) Firms	(3) Government	(4) Financial intermediaries	(5) Central bank	(6) Rest of the world	Total
(1) Goods and services	$-S_p$	I_p	$(I_g - S_g)$	–	–	CAB^*	0
(2) Money base	dM_h^+	dM_f^+	–	dM_i^+	dM_r^-	–	0
(3) Bank deposits	dD_h^+	dD_f^+	–	dD_i^-	–	dD_*^+	0
(4) Bonds	dB_h^+	dB_f^+	dB_g^-	dB_i^+	dB_r^+	dB_*^+	0
(5) Equities	dQ_h^+	dQ_f^-	–	–	–	dQ_*^+	0
(6) Other debt instruments	dH_h^+	dH_f^-	–	dH_i^+	–	dH_*^+	0
(7) Foreign currency reserves	–	–	–	–	dR_r^+	dR_*^-	0
Total	0	0	0	0	0	0	0

Figure 2.4 Saving, investment and financial flows in an open economy

and financial transactions take place (the rows) as well as the six sectors (the columns). All rows and columns must sum to zero according to national and external accounting principles as well as balance sheet constraints. Summing across the first row

$$(I_p - S_p) + (I_g - S_g) + CAB^* \tag{2.10}$$

Hence

$$(I_p - S_p) + (Ig - S_g) = NFI = CAD = KAS \tag{2.11}$$

if public and private investment exceeds domestic saving as derived earlier. The remaining rows show, in simplified form, the various financial markets.

In the second row, changes in sectoral holdings of the money base (consisting of coin, banknotes and cash balances of the banks at the central bank) must reflect *ex post* changes in financial asset and liability positions. In Figure 4.2 assets are shown by superscript '+' and liabilities by superscript '−'. Assuming neither the government nor foreigners demand domestically issued base money, this row reveals that an increase in the base money supply, as a liability of the central bank, (dM_r) must be matched by a rise in money base held as an asset in the portfolios of firms (dM_f), households (dM_h) and financial intermediaries (dM_i). Hence

$$dM_f + dM_h + dM_i = dM_r \tag{2.12}$$

In the third row, a change in demand deposits with financial intermediaries can arise as deposits by households (dD_h), firms (dD_f) and foreign entities (dD_*) in financial intermediaries increase. The increased asset positions of households, firms and foreign entities is matched by a rise in the intermediaries' consolidated liability position such that

$$dD_f + dD_h + dD_* = dD_i \tag{2.13}$$

The fourth row simply shows that changes in the growth of government securities on issue, which are the liabilities of the central government, must be matched by increased holdings of bonds in the portfolios of the agents in the other five sectors. That is

$$dB_g + dB_f + dB_i + dB_r + dB_* = dB_g \qquad (2.14)$$

Row five reveals that additional capital accumulation by private firms funded through the sale of equities must be absorbed as assets by households (dQ_h) and foreign investors (dQ_*). It is assumed that neither financial institutions nor the official sector is permitted to buy shares in domestic enterprises. Hence

$$Q_f = dQ_h + dQ_* \qquad (2.15)$$

If the enterprise issuing equities is a subsidiary of a foreign firm and new share issues are exclusively taken up by foreign buyers, then the item dE_* would be classified in the capital account as *direct* foreign investment in the economy. The distinction between direct and portfolio foreign investment is further discussed shortly.

The other main way of raising financial capital is through borrowing as shown in row six. This form of financing real capital accumulation also appears as a liability of domestic firms, but of course does not provide the lenders of funds with the same legal claim to ownership of domestic firms, as is the case with equity participation.

Firms may borrow either directly from households (dH_h) or foreigners (dH_*)(for instance, through the issue of company debentures) or alternatively they may borrow indirectly from those sectors through financial intermediaries (dH_i). Therefore

$$dH_f = dH_h + dH_* + dH_i \qquad (2.16)$$

If resident households provide insufficient funds to finance domestically-located firms' investment activity, funds will be sought from abroad in the form of borrowings or equity participation. Though equity issues are usually denominated in domestic currency, foreign debt may be denominated in either domestic or foreign currency.

The last row shows the extent of foreign exchange market intervention undertaken by the central bank or the change in the stock of its official reserve assets (dR_*). Official reserve assets are by and large held in the form of financial assets previously issued by foreign governments and foreign central banks, but also include gold bullion. Hence $dR_r = dR_*$. Under a fixed exchange system, dR_*, as the change in the stock of official reserves, provides a measure of a nation's overall balance of payments position but, this measure of external balance effectively becomes redundant under a floating exchange rate system.[1] Instead, under a float, the change in official reserves provides a measure of the extent to which the central bank intervenes to prevent appreciation or perhaps induce depreciation of the exchange rate itself.

Next consider the columns of the matrix which present the budget constraints of all six sectors. In column one, households dispose of their saving by increasing holdings of cash balances, (dM_h), cash deposits (dD_h), bonds (dD_h), equities (dQ_h) and interest bearing securities (dH_f). The total increase is the change in household wealth (dW_h). So

$$S_p = dM_h + dD_h + dB_h + dQ_h + dH_h = dW_h \qquad (2.17)$$

Firms (column two) produce goods and services for sale in markets and finance additional net capital accumulation by issuing securities as claims in the form of equities (dQ_f)and debt (dH_f) or by running down cash balances (dM_f) and bank deposits (dD_f), or by selling bond holdings (dB_f).[2] The total increase is the change in the capital stock of enterprises, dK_p. Hence

$$I_p = dQ_f + dH_f - dM_f - dD_f - dB_f = dK_p \qquad (2.18)$$

Column three is the government's budget constraint. The government sector includes 'departments of State', but in practice often excludes public sector business enterprises which are usually grouped with private firms for data collection purposes. If there is a budget deficit, there is an excess of government investment spending (I_g) over public saving (S_g), and this deficit is financed by issuing government bonds. The government's net financing requirement is therefore

$$dB_g = I_g - S_g \qquad (2.19)$$

The financial sector (column four) includes licensed trading, saving and development banks and non-bank financial institutions which incur liabilities and acquire financial assets. For financial intermediaries, the budget constraint is

$$dM_i + dB_i + dH_i = dD_i \qquad (2.20)$$

which states that changes in this sector's holdings of cash reserves (dM_i), bonds (dB_i) and its consolidated loan position (dH_i), all recorded on the credit side of the balance sheet, are equivalent to the change in deposits (dD_i), recorded on the debit side.

The fifth column is the central bank's budget constraint. It shows that the supply of base money can only be increased (dM_r) through the central bank's open market purchases of bonds (dB_r) or by purchases of foreign exchange or securities in the foreign exchange market. Hence foreign exchange market intervention has monetary consequences and may therefore be undertaken by the central bank as a means of expanding or contracting the money supply for macroeconomic stabilisation purposes. However, if influencing the exchange rate is the sole objective of intervention (dR_r), the change in the money base (dM_r) must be offset, or sterilised, through open market operations by an equivalent change in the central bank's bond holdings (dB_r). For instance, if the central bank buys foreign exchange to prevent appreciation of the exchange rate, it must simultaneously sell government bonds from its portfolio to prevent an unintended monetary expansion.

Finally, the sixth column shows the composition of net capital inflow from the perspective of the rest of the world, classified by financial instruments. Under a pure float, there is no central bank intervention in the foreign exchange market, so $dR_r = dR_* = 0$. As shown previously the rest of the world's net capital outflow is equivalent to the domestic economy's *CAD* or *NFI*.

NFI therefore arises because foreigners use their surplus saving to purchase equities (dQ_*) and debt instruments (dH_*) issued by domestic firms, bonds (dB_*) issued by the government and by depositing funds with financial institutions (dD_*). Hence

$$NFI = dQ_* + dH_* + dB_* + dD_* \qquad (2.21)$$

If the exchange rate is fixed or if the central bank intervenes in the foreign exchange markets, the change recorded in the stock of official reserve assets (dR_r) also changes the liability position of the rest of the world (dR_*). Any rundown of reserves which may be the result of a central bank strategy to appreciate the currency, or prevent it from depreciating, therefore augments the existing capital inflow which is financing the nation's *CAD*.

If the government's budget is balanced $(I_g - S_g = dB_g = 0)$ and there is a pure float $(dR_r = dR_* = 0)$ it follows from the matrix that foreigners can finance, through purchases of domestic equity, debt instruments and bank deposits, that much more private domestic capital accumulation, that is

$$dD_* + dQ_* + dH_* = dK_p \tag{2.22}$$

A further distinction drawn about *NFI* is that between *portfolio* investment and *direct* investment. Portfolio or indirect investment refers to ordinary foreign purchases of domestic debt or equity claims whereas direct foreign investment includes investment which suggests significant foreign control over the management of resident firms and their real assets including subsidiaries of foreign firms. For measurement purposes, foreign ownership of at least 10 per cent of ordinary shares or equivalent equity interest in an enterprise is defined as constituting significant influence. Schematically, the distinction is as shown in Figure 2.5.

2.2.2 Inflation-adjusted current account

Unlike other macroeconomic variables such as the national accounting aggregates, wages, the money supply, interest rates and exchange rates, external accounts data are not normally adjusted for the distortionary effects of domestic inflation. So, a method for adjusting *CAB*s for domestic inflation is presented in what follows.

The counterpart of a *CAB* over any time period should in principle equal an *ex post* change in financial liabilities to the rest of the world which can take the form of either interest-bearing liabilities or equities. Hence, a comprehensive set of external accounts should incorporate stocks as well as flows and record the balance of financial indebtedness as well as payments.

Under a floating exchange rate regime and with some degree of capital mobility, current account deficits should be matched on the capital side of the external accounts by growth in the nominal

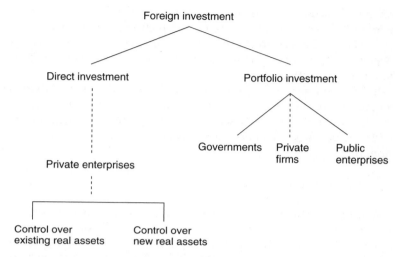

Figure 2.5   Direct vs portfolio foreign investment

domestic value of the external liabilities of all domestic sectors. From a supply of funds perspective, there is no *a priori* reason to accept that debt is a more useful a form of finance than equity, although foreign debt requires servicing through interest payments, while foreign equity capital must be serviced eventually through dividend payments. Nonetheless, foreign debt and equity obligations are usually denominated in different currencies with debt often valued in foreign currency, whereas equities issued by local enterprises, yet purchased by foreigners, are invariably denominated in domestic currency.

The difference between foreign liabilities and residents' foreign asset holdings determines the nation's foreign investment position. According to international convention, the balance of payments accounts as measured in domestic currency over any period excludes capital gains or losses arising from movements in the market value of foreign assets and foreign liabilities over the same time frame. Moreover, apart from capital gains and losses, there will be another valuation effect due to exchange rate movements affecting the domestic currency value of those external assets and liabilities denominated in foreign currency. Hence

$$T + i_f eH + i_h B + lQ + t + EeH = \frac{d}{dt}(B + eH + Q) \qquad (2.23)$$

where T is the goods and services trade balance; i_f is the nominal interest rate on foreign currency denominated external debt (H) ; i_h is the nominal interest rate paid on home currency denominated external debt (B); e is the effective exchange rate, l is the dividend rate on foreign owned equities (Q) ; t is other transfers; and E is exchange rate depreciation, $\frac{de}{dt}/e$.

In an inflationary environment, the real value or burden of these foreign obligations denominated in home currency falls at a rate equal to the domestic inflation rate and, consistent with the Fisher real interest rate effect, part of annual interest payments effectively compensates lenders for the erosion in the value of their principal. Hence, the inflation segment of interest received is not really additional income earned by creditors. Yet, under existing external accounting procedures, all interest actually paid to foreigners appears in the current account. That part attributable to inflation should however be recorded in the capital account. For a debtor nation, although domestic inflation erodes the burden of net external liabilities denominated in foreign currency, exchange rate depreciation augments it. Therefore, over any period, the real change in the value of external obligations invoiced in foreign currency is the nominal change less inflation plus depreciation.

More formally, if we deflate the change in the stock of an economy's outstanding external liabilities by its price level, P, we obtain

$$
\begin{aligned}
\frac{d}{dt}\frac{(B + eH + Q)}{P} &= \frac{\left(\frac{dB}{dt} + EeH + e.\frac{dH}{dt} + \frac{dQ}{dt}\right)P - (B + eH + Q)\frac{dP}{dt}}{P^2} \\
&= \frac{\left(\frac{dB}{dt} + EeH + e.\frac{dH}{dt} + \frac{dQ}{dt}\right) - (B + eH + Q)\pi}{P} \qquad (2.24)
\end{aligned}
$$

where π is the rate of domestic inflation, $\frac{dP}{dt}/P$.

Substituting equation (2.23) into (2.24)

$$\frac{d}{dt}\frac{(B+eH+Q)}{P} = \frac{(T+i_f eH + i_h B + lQ + t + seH) - (B+eH+Q)\pi}{P}$$

$$= \frac{(T+t)}{P} + (i_h - \pi)\frac{B}{P} + (i_f - \pi + E)\frac{eH}{P}$$

$$+ (l-\pi)\frac{Q}{P} \qquad (2.25)$$

Equation (2.25) provides an expression for the inflation-adjusted current account balance. On the basis of the above methodology, the adjusted measures of economies' external imbalances can be significantly lower than actual values because recorded net capital inflow is effectively overestimated under inflationary conditions. As an example, Australia's inflation-adjusted imbalance averaged around 2.3 per cent of GDP in the 1980s compared with an average of 4.9 per cent for the nominal imbalance over the same period.

Inflation-adjusted measures of external imbalance therefore provide a measure of the extent of the real transfer of capital which takes place between current account surplus and current account deficit nations. They may also reveal by how much the real domestic capital stock can be greater, or potentially less, because of net international inflows or outflows of saving. Alternatively, taking the case of a deficit country, the inflation-adjusted *CAB* for given investment opportunities measures the volume of consumption which domestic residents would have to forego in order to attain the same real increase in their capital stock.

2.2.3 National wealth accounting

So far, the main focus of this chapter has been the interrelationship between domestic and international flow magnitudes. An economy's performance is usually assessed in terms of flow measures of national output and income since changes in these aggregates can affect employment and the price level. Reflecting this, traditional open economy macroeconomic theory deals extensively with flow transactions within and between nations. However, the associated economy-wide stock measures are also important since these permit measurement of national wealth in open economies.

When making international comparisons, output levels per head for instance are used as indicators of economic development. However, is an economy whose real GDP is, say, $300 billion and whose real national net worth, or national wealth, a stock measure, is $1000 billion, necessarily better off than an economy of similar population with a lower GDP, say $290 billion, but significantly higher wealth, say $1200 billion? This example suggests conventional flow income measures should be augmented with stock measures of national wealth, to give a more complete picture of macroeconomic welfare, particularly for highly internationally indebted economies.

The attention presently given to aggregate flows in the system of national accounts undoubtedly stems from the strong influence of Keynesian macroeconomic theory which stressed consumption and investment flows as determinants of aggregate demand and hence of employment and unemployment. One possible reason why macroeconomic stocks have received relatively little attention in macroeconomic analysis may relate to the presumption in much Keynesian analysis that, as a rule, the market valuation of capital assets is likely to be inefficient. As Keynes (1936) himself argued for instance, stock-markets and presumably also property markets were subject to highly speculative influences and in effect were best ignored for policy purposes. This is sharply at odds with more recent developments in the finance literature. Orthodox finance theory presupposes that asset markets are not inherently irrational but instead generally tend to be efficient in their use of information about economic fundamentals.

All the while, however, stocks have been important in other areas of macroeconomic analysis and policy. For instance, the market price value of the capital stock, relative to its replacement value, has been central to theories of investment behaviour[3] and the capital stock itself plays a major role in the growth literature, both old and new.

To estimate open economies' wealth positions, it is necessary to construct national balance sheets which should be an integral part of national accounting. They are tied directly to aggregate flows through the national capital account which records saving and investment aggregates, these in turn having been derived from the income and product accounts. While total domestic investment equals domestic saving plus net capital inflow, national net worth or wealth equals tangible assets less foreign liabilities. As complements to the flow national income measures, national balance sheets complete the full

Table 2.1   Stylised open economy balance sheet

Assets		Liabilities (claims on assets)
Consumer durables		Foreign liabilities
Capital stock		Private
Private		Public
Public		
Foreign assets		
Private		
Public		Residents' net worth (national wealth)
Total Assets	=	Total Claims

System of National Accounts (SNA), as actually recommended by the United Nations. They should include all assets and liabilities which have market values and can be expressed in dollar terms. In a globally integrated economic system, market values should, ideally, reflect the prices bid for domestic assets if these assets were offered for sale on international goods, services and financial markets.

Taking the case of an internationally indebted open economy, national net wealth, is simply defined as the excess of the value of residents' assets, (comprised of consumer durables,[4] the tangible capital stock, and foreign assets), over external liabilities, as shown in the stylised balance sheet of Table 2.1. National wealth, as a stock measure, is conceptually equivalent to residents' net worth or the difference between the tangible and foreign assets which residents own, offset by foreigners' claims to those assets. National wealth measures the value of resources potentially available for future consumption. In practice, national wealth statements should include all non-human assets and claims at market prices.

Human capital is not included in the above balance sheet because, in practice, human capital is very difficult to quantify with any precision. Omission of human capital is also justifiable because claims to human capital can not be bought and sold within, or between, free societies in the same manner as financial and tangible assets. This is not to deny the macroeconomic significance of the human capital stock however, whose value could well be a large multiple of the tangible capital stock.

2.2.4 Capital gains and national income

The sources of growth in national wealth for an open economy can be shown in an expression that includes an explicit role for international investment flows. In deriving the expression, all stock and flow variables are presumed to be adjusted for the effects of goods and services inflation and are net of capital stock depreciation (or consumption of fixed capital).

Starting with the assets side of the national balance sheet, it is possible to relate the real value of total assets at an earlier date (h) to the value of total assets at a later date (j), as well as to other accumulation and valuation changes which occurred between these points in time. Hence

$$K_j(t) + A_j^*(t) = [K_h(t) + \int_h^j I(t)dt + \int_h^j D(t)dt + v(t)]$$

$$+ [A_h^*(t) + \int_h^j I_A^*(t)dt + v(t)^*] \qquad (2.26)$$

where $K_{h,j}(t)$ is the market value at dates h,j of the tangible capital stock located domestically; $A^*_{h,j}(t)$ is the market value at dates h,j of the foreign assets of residents; $I(t)$ is domestic investment net of consumption of fixed capital between h and j; $D(t)$ is domestic expenditure on consumer durables between h and j; $v(t)$ is capital gains on all domestic assets between h and j; $I_A^*(t)$ is foreign investment abroad between h and j; and $v^*(t)$ is capital gains on foreign assets between dates h and j.

Now, the definition of net worth relating national assets and external liabilities is

$$NW_{hj}(t) \equiv K_{hj}(t) + D_{hj}(t) + A^*_{hj}(t) - F_{hj}(t) \qquad (2.27)$$

where $NW(t)$ is net worth and $F(t)$ is gross external liabilities for the host country. Substituting (2.27) into (2.26)

$$NW_j(t) + F_j(t) = NW_h(t) + F_h(t) + \int_h^j I(t).dt + v(t) + \int_h^j D(t).dt$$

$$+ \int_h^j I_A^*(t).dt + v^*(t) \tag{2.28}$$

Therefore, the stock change in the value of net worth (*dNW*) between dates *h* and *j* is

$$dNW(t) = NW_j(t) - NW_h(t) = F_h(t) - F_j(t) + \int_h^j I(t).dt$$

$$+ \int_h^j I_A^*(t).dt + \int_h^j D(t).dt + v(t) + v^*(t) \tag{2.29}$$

International capital flows can be introduced by recalling that net foreign investment is the difference between gross capital inflow and gross capital outflow between two dates. Also, according to *SNA* convention, external account flows exclude all capital gains and losses on the face value of stock claims. Hence

$$\int_h^j NFI(t).dt = \int_h^j I_h^*(t).dt - \int_h^j I_A^*(t).dt$$

$$= [F_j(t) - F_h(t) - z(t)] - [A_j^*(t) + A_h^*(t) - v^*(t)] \tag{2.30}$$

where *NFI(t)* is net foreign investment in the home country; $I_h^*(t)$ is gross foreign capital inflow; and *z(t)* is capital gains on domestic assets to which foreigners hold direct claims.

Using (2.30) to substitute for I_A^* in (2.29), it follows algebraically that

$$dNW(t) = \underbrace{\int_h^j I(t).dt + \int_h^j D(t).dt - \int_h^j NFI(t).dt}_{\text{net accumulation}} + \underbrace{v(t) + v^*(t) - z(t)}_{\text{net capital gains}}$$

$$\tag{2.31}$$

Equation (2.31) reveals the fundamental sources of growth in national wealth, between dates h and j. National wealth rises because of greater accumulation, capital gains or both. Amongst other things, this expression implies that if additional domestic investment is fully financed by external borrowing, then macroeconomic welfare improves whenever the value of the additional real capital exceeds the value of the extra foreign debt.

Using the conventional definition of national saving (gross national product less total consumption) which is exclusive of spending on consumer durables, it can be shown easily that the accumulation term above is simply equal to national saving between h and j. This is because the integral of *NFI* is also the difference between the integrals for investment and the conventional saving measure, that is

$$\int_h^j NFI(t).dt = \int_h^j I(t).dt - \int_h^j S(t).dt \tag{2.32}$$

The external liabilities of nations, particularly in the form of debt, as opposed to equity, are often considered in absolute value terms and in isolation, and have seemingly assumed an importance of themselves. Alternatively, external liabilities are often expressed in relation to GDP, for purposes of international comparison, although such measures are really devoid of economic content. The widespread attention afforded to external liabilities can however be misleading when interpreting the overall performance of open economies. To remedy this, a total approach to measuring internationally saleable assets should be adopted by central statistical agencies. This means extending existing techniques to include measurement of the domestic capital stock at market values. Routinely published national wealth accounts would then provide a more complete picture of international macroeconomic welfare, notwithstanding the many practical difficulties likely to arise in valuing nations' tradeable assets and liabilities.

2.3 Exchange rates

Exchange rates and how they are managed are central to the international adjustment process modelled in subsequent chapters. When referring to 'the' exchange rate in international monetary models, it is often implicitly assumed that the relevant exchange rate is the effective, or trade weighted, exchange rate. The standard formula for a trade weighted exchange rate index (TWI) is

$$TWI(t) = 100 \times \prod_{i=1}^{n} \varepsilon_i(t)^{w_i} \qquad (2.33)$$

where n is the number of currencies in the basket (indexed by i), $\varepsilon_1(t)$ is the value of currency i in terms of the domestic currency at time t and w_i is the weight assigned to currency i. Note however that as is normal in the academic exchange rate literature, the nominal exchange rate, e, will usually be defined hereafter as the value of the domestic currency in terms of the foreign currency, in contrast to its reciprocal, ε, the market definition employed in the above equation. The weights in the *TWI* are calculated as the sum of exports *(X)* to and imports *(M)* from country i as a proportion of the total amount of an economy's international trade. Hence

$$w_i = \frac{X_i + M_i}{\sum_{i=l}^{n}(X_i + M_i)} \qquad (2.34)$$

The formulation in (2.33), a fixed weight Laspeyres index, raises several important issues in index number theory. For instance, such an index may not be useful for evaluating long-term exchange rate trends to the extent that it fails to reflect accurately the changing nature and country composition of an economy's international trade. To avoid this problem, updated weights for the index can then be compared to earlier values by using a 'chaining' technique that systematically rebases the index using the latest trade flow data.

The above indices can then be adjusted for relative inflation rates, thus obtaining a set of 'real' capital weighted exchange rate indices. From equation (2.33), the inflation-adjusted index is given as

$$RTWI(t) = 100 \times \prod_{i=l}^{n} \left(\frac{P(t)}{P_i^*(t)} \varepsilon_i(t) \right)^{w_i} \qquad (2.35)$$

where ε_i is defined as in (2.33), $P(t)$ and $P_i^*(t)$ are the domestic and foreign (country i) price indices at time t.

It is also possible to devise effective exchange rate indices based on the flow and stock entries recorded on the financial side of the balance of payments accounts. For instance, instead of using trade weights, it is possible to construct 'capital weighted' exchange rate measures using international investment data.[5]

2.4 Conclusion

Taken as a whole, a nation's international transactions must always balance. Under a float, exchange rates themselves move to eliminate any excess demand or supply of currencies on the foreign exchanges, whereas the central bank soaks up any excess currency supply or demand through its exchange market intervention when exchange rates are officially managed. Under a float, if one particular category of external transactions rises or falls, an equilibrating mechanism leads to an offset in other external account categories.

For example, if there is increased demand for an economy's financial assets, the additional foreign investment raises the capital account surplus which may strengthen the exchange rate, with offsetting implications for the trade balance. In sum, the current and capital account imbalances are jointly determined at the point where the net demand for foreign funds on one side matches the net supply on the other with the exchange rate proximately performing the equilibrating role.

The 'balance of payments' as such does not refer to the notion of the balance of payments as understood if the exchange rate is fixed. With a fixed exchange rate, the balance of payments is essentially the measure of the change in the central bank's holdings of foreign exchange reserves. Under the Bretton Woods system of exchange rate management nations' balance of payments problems most often involved unsustainable rundowns in official international reserve assets. Such holdings were necessary to maintain the value of the currency in the face of a shortfall between residents' demand for foreign currency arising, for example, as a consequence of the demand for imports, and the supply of foreign currency provided to residents by foreigners as occurred, for example, when exports were sold. When that system prevailed, international capital markets were far less sophisticated and financial capital flows were less voluminous; balance of payments deficits therefore usually arose for current account reasons though there were substantial international capital flows. Nevertheless, availability of central banks' reserves represented the ultimate external constraint on an economy's performance.

In contrast, the floating exchange rate system in operation from the early 1970s, almost by definition has not depended on direct foreign exchange market intervention by the monetary authorities to maintain any particular exchange rate. Under the purest of exchange rate floats, the overall balance of payments of a nation should in practice be zero with the exchange rate itself bearing all the pressure of external adjustment. Hence, in what follows the focus will not be the overall balance of payments as the measure of central bank intervention in the foreign exchange markets but the two matching sides of the external accounts – the current account and the capital account.

The macroeconomic notion of 'external imbalance' as a constraint was widely employed during the fixed exchange rate era, to describe external account outcomes characterised by either unsustainable rundowns or excessive accumulations of foreign currency reserves by central banks. However, with the progressive dismantling of capital controls, along with the shift to more flexible exchange rates, the old notion of external imbalance as a reserve constraint lost its former meaning. Nonetheless, the term persists in the literature and in popular usage but now generally refers to current account outcomes. Often, however, the term still conveys the implication that some form of remedial macroeconomic policy action is necessary.

However, as argued in later chapters, such an understanding is misplaced under current circumstances. Therefore, whenever the term 'external imbalance' is used in discussing developments under floating exchange rates, it is simply meant to describe the current account outcome, capital account outcome, or net foreign investment position; it is not meant to convey a state of macroeconomic disequilibrium begging a particular macroeconomic policy response.

3
Early Balance of Payments Models

This chapter surveys well-known early models of balance of payments adjustment. Aspects of these models provide important background to more recent approaches and contain insights that remain relevant today. The different approaches that emerged are presented largely in order of their chronological appearance. It becomes clear that interpretations of the theoretical and policy significance of the balance of payments and the external adjustment process evolved in line with changes in the rules governing the international financial system.

In the beginning, the classical adjustment mechanism sought to explain the dynamics of reaching external equilibrium for economies that had their exchange rates fixed under the gold standard. After the abandonment of the gold standard, the elasticities approach to trade account adjustment became popular and was heavily influenced by the partial approach of neo-classicism with its emphasis on changing relative prices of exports and imports, yet under circumstances where the exchange rate could be used as an instrument of policy. After the emergence of macroeconomics as a distinct sub-discipline from the late 1930s, economy-wide approaches to international adjustment again became popular as reflected in the absorption-related approaches of the 1950s.

The macroeconomic approaches which developed in the Bretton Woods era, for instance, did so in an environment where strict exchange controls over the movement of financial capital were in force which effectively segmented financial markets, making capital markets unresponsive to international interest rate differentials. Hence the models of this era used fixed exchange rates and capital immobility as starting assumptions, such that the current account became the focus of balance of payments analysis to the neglect of the capital account. During this time, the monetary approach to the balance of payments also emerged in parallel with the Monetarists' rejection of the Keynesian emphasis on the expenditure aggregates, rather than monetary factors, in the closed economy literature.

It was not until the 1960s, by which time economies' capital markets had become more internationally integrated, that the significance of capital mobility was fully recognized and explicitly modelled in the Keynesian inspired Mundell-Fleming model. This approach proved popular as it could just as easily model macroeconomic policy in an open economy under the generalized floating exchange rate regime from the early 1970s onwards as it could under fixed rates. It is outlined in a later chapter.

3.1   The classical approach

The open economy literature has traditionally focused on the trade and current account imbalance as a measure of balance of payments disequilibrium or external imbalance. What 'external balance' means today under conditions where international borrowing and lending is freely permitted and many exchange rates float has become quite ambiguous. Yet, it was clear to the ancient Mercantilist school of thought, popular in England between the fifteenth and mid-eighteenth centuries, that external balance meant a trade surplus.

The Mercantilist position on the balance of payments is best captured in Thomas Mun's (1664) pamphlet entitled 'England's Treasure by Foreign Trade, or the Balance of our Foreign Trade is the Rule of Our Treasure' in which he proposed that: 'The ordinary means therefore to increase our wealth and treasure is by Foreign Trade, wherein we must even observe this rule: to sell more to strangers yearly than we consume of theirs in value'. Why trade surpluses were, of themselves, considered desirable was probably because it was thought that the accumulation of specie raised national wealth. The benefits or otherwise of particular outcomes on the trade account continue to generate debate. Indeed, Mercantilist instincts survive today to the extent that external balance is sometimes interpreted as achieving a current account surplus as an appropriate end goal of macroeconomic policy.

3.1.1   The basic model

Using a macroeconomic argument, David Hume discredited the Mercantilists' policy objective of actively pursuing a trade surplus and, in so doing, proposed the first theory of balance of payments adjustment. In his classic essay 'Of the Balance of Trade' (1752) Hume outlined what became known as the 'price-specie-flow' mechanism under the gold standard.

The gold standard operated on the basis that the value of national currencies or base monies was defined in terms of gold. With gold as the internationally agreed standard of value, this implied that currencies were therefore defined in terms of each other. As payments imbalances arose, gold reserves could be physically transported across national borders to settle international accounts for goods bought and sold. Hume argued that under the gold standard, a trade surplus would certainly induce gold inflow but that this would also increase the domestic money supply. By virtue of the quantity theory of money, the domestic price level would then rise, worsening competitiveness which would subsequently reverse the trade imbalance.

Schematically

	(1)		(2)
	Trade surplus (deficit)	→	Gold inflow (outflow)
	(3)		(4)
→	Money supply increase (decrease)	→	Domestic price level increase (decrease)
	(5)		(6)
→	Fall (rise) in competitiveness	→	Reversal of trade surplus (deficit)

Importantly, the linkages suggested that trade account imbalances were eventually self correcting, thus obviating the need for economic policy responses to balance of payments disturbances.

Nonetheless, several factors could impede the external adjustment process as proposed by Hume. For instance, the link between stages (3) and (4) has been the subject of continued controversy, particularly its relevance for short period analysis. Furthermore, the link between stages (5) and (6) also only worked with constant foreign price levels and the absence of retaliatory trade action on the part of foreign governments. The exact nature of the relative price conditions necessary at stage (5) to alter the trade imbalance at stage (6) later preoccupied the advocates of the so called elasticities approach.

3.1.2 Limitations

This approach can be criticised on the grounds that it implicitly assumed wages and prices were fully flexible both upwards and downwards and that full employment of resources therefore prevailed. This assumption was of course subsequently at the heart of Keynes' (1936) challenge of classical orthodoxy.

Misplaced Mercantilist doctrine about the paramount importance of the trade account also provided Hume's contemporary, Adam Smith, with a motive for writing *The Wealth of Nations* (1776) in which Smith espoused the case for minimal intervention by government in most spheres of economic activity including trade with foreigners. Smith rejected the thrust of Mercantilist precepts and policy prescriptions, about the need for State intervention to improve economic welfare, yet his classic book does not acknowledge the price-specie-flow model, nor anything resembling it. Instead, Smith emphasised the gains from international trade which hitherto had been largely considered a zero-sum game. On the question of external imbalance, Smith commented:

> Nothing ... can be more absurd than this whole doctrine of the balance of trade ... When two places trade with one another, this doctrine supposes that, if the balance be even, neither of them either loses or gains; but if it leans in any degree to one side, that one of them loses, and the other gains in proportion to its declension from the exact equilibrium. Both suppositions are false... that trade which, without force or constraint, is naturally carried on between any two places, is always advantageous ... to both.
>
> (Adam Smith, Bk. IV, Ch. III, part 2, para. 2)

This Smithian theme reemerges when the gains from international trade in saving are considered in the next chapter.

Although it was the ruling orthodoxy until the abandonment of the gold standard in the early 1930s, whereafter it lost its immediate relevance, it was the Humean adjustment mechanism which profoundly influenced subsequent international monetary theory and balance of payments analysis. Indeed, as becomes clear later in this chapter, many elements of the approach resurfaced intact in the monetary approach to the balance of payments which became popular in the 1960s.

3.2 The elasticities approach

While the classical approach was the centrepiece of external adjustment theory during the neo-classical Marginalist revolution in economics of the late nineteenth century, Marginalism, with its emphasis on partial, as opposed to general equilibrium analysis, inspired a new approach to the balance of payments termed the 'elasticities approach'. With the trade balance still the main focus, the elasticities approach explained the response of exports and imports, not under the classical conditions where the exchange rate was fixed under the gold standard and domestic price levels varied, but where domestic price levels were fixed and the exchange rate itself could vary. In common with the classical approach, the elasticities approach did not allow changing national income levels to affect trade flows. Instead, it sought to establish the conditions necessary for changes in competitiveness to improve trade imbalances.

In essence, this perspective centred on the response to exchange rate changes of the trade balance in foreign exchange terms, since trade deficits ultimately had to be financed by depleting official foreign exchange reserves.

3.2.1 The basic model

The elasticities approach addressed the conditions necessary for devaluations to improve trade balances. These necessary conditions can be derived as follows. The change in the trade balance is expressed as

$$dT^* = dX^* - dM^* \tag{3.1}$$

where asterisks here denote foreign exchange values.

Starting with the export side of the trade account, X^* can be further expressed as

$$X^* = Q_x P_x^* \tag{3.2}$$

where Q_x is the volume of exports and P_x^* is the foreign price of exports. If e is the price of foreign exchange, then

$$P_x = eP_x^* \qquad (3.3)$$

where P_x is the domestic price of exports.

The elasticity of supply of exports with respect to price is

$$\varepsilon_x = \frac{dQ_x}{Q_x} \Big/ \frac{dP_x}{P_x} \qquad (3.4)$$

and the elasticity of demand for exports on the part of foreigners is

$$\eta_x = \frac{-dQ_x}{Q_x} \Big/ \frac{dP_x^*}{P_x^*} \qquad (3.5)$$

From (3.3)

$$\frac{dP_x}{P_x} = \frac{de}{e} + \frac{dP_x^*}{P_x^*} \qquad (3.6)$$

Substituting (3.6) into (3.4) we obtain

$$\varepsilon_x = \frac{dQ_x}{Q_x} \Big/ \left(\frac{dP_x^*}{P_x^*} + \frac{de}{e} \right) \qquad (3.7)$$

Using (3.5) we also obtain

$$\frac{dQ_x}{Q_x} = -\eta \frac{dP_x^*}{P_x^*} \qquad (3.8)$$

Substituting (3.8) into (3.7)

$$\frac{dP_x^*}{P} = \left(\frac{-\varepsilon_x}{\eta_x + \varepsilon_x} \right) \frac{de}{e} < 0 \qquad (3.9)$$

Substituting (3.9) back into (3.5)

$$\frac{dQ_x}{Q_x} = \left(\frac{\eta_x \varepsilon_x}{\eta_x + \varepsilon_x} \right) \frac{de}{e} > 0 \qquad (3.10)$$

The proportionate change in the value of exports is

$$\frac{dX^*}{X^*} = \frac{dP_x^*}{P_x} + \frac{dQ_x}{Q_x} \qquad (3.11)$$

Substituting from (3.9) and (3.10) yields

$$\frac{dX^*}{X^*} = \frac{\varepsilon_x(\eta_x - 1)}{(\eta_x + \varepsilon_x)} \frac{de}{e} \qquad (3.12)$$

On the imports side, the foreign currency value of imports is

$$M^* = Q_M P_M^* \qquad (3.13)$$

where Q_M is the volume of imports and P_M^* is the foreign price of imports.

The domestic price of imports is

$$P_M = e P_M^* \qquad (3.14)$$

The elasticity of supply of imports with respect to price is

$$\varepsilon_M = \frac{dQ_M}{Q_M} \bigg/ \frac{dP_M^*}{P_M^*} \qquad (3.15)$$

The elasticity of demand for imports domestically is

$$\eta_M = \frac{-dQ_M}{Q_M} \bigg/ \frac{dP_M}{P_M} \qquad (3.16)$$

From (3.14),

$$\frac{dP_M}{P_M} = \frac{dP_M^*}{P_M^*} + \frac{de}{e} \qquad (3.17)$$

Substitute (3.17) into (3.16)

$$\eta_M = \frac{-dQ_M}{Q_M} \bigg/ \left(\frac{dP_M^*}{P_M} + \frac{de}{e}\right) \qquad (3.18)$$

From (3.15)

$$\frac{dQ_M}{Q_M} = \varepsilon_M \frac{dP_M^*}{P_M^*} \qquad (3.19)$$

Substitute (3.19) into (3.18) we obtain

$$\frac{dP_M^*}{P_M^*} = \left(\frac{-\eta_M}{\eta_M + \varepsilon_M}\right) \frac{de}{e} \qquad (3.20)$$

Using (3.20) in (3.15) and solving for the proportionate change in the quantity of imports

$$\frac{dQ_M}{Q_M} = \frac{-\varepsilon_M \eta_M}{(\varepsilon_M + \eta_M)} \frac{de}{e} \qquad (3.21)$$

Now the proportionate change in the value of imports is

$$\frac{dM^*}{M^*} = \frac{dP_M^*}{P_M^*} + \frac{dQ_M}{Q_M} \qquad (3.22)$$

Substituting from (3.20) and (3.21)

$$\frac{dM^*}{M^*} = \frac{\eta_M(\varepsilon_M + 1)}{(\varepsilon_M + \eta_M)} \frac{de}{e} \qquad (3.23)$$

Substituting the expressions in terms of elasticities derived for proportionate changes in exports (3.12) and proportionate changes in imports (3.23) into equation (3.1)

$$dT^* = \left(X^* \frac{\varepsilon_x(\eta_x - 1)}{(\eta_x + \varepsilon_x)} + M^* \frac{\eta_M(1 + \varepsilon_M)}{(\eta_M + \varepsilon_M)} \right) \frac{de}{e} \qquad (3.24)$$

With balanced trade, $X^* = M^*$, so that a devaluation (de/e) only improves the trade balance if

$$\frac{\varepsilon_x(\eta_x - 1)}{(\eta_x + \varepsilon_x)} + \frac{(\eta_M(1 + \varepsilon_M))}{(\eta_M + \varepsilon_M)} > 0 \qquad (3.25)$$

where, redefining for convenience, ε_x is the elasticity of the domestic supply of exports, η_x is the elasticity of foreign demand for exports, ε_M is the elasticity of the supply of imports and η_M is the elasticity of domestic demand for imports.

From (3.25) we can derive special conditions. For instance, consider first the case of a small economy facing an infinitely elastic foreign demand for its exports ($\eta_x = \infty$) and an infinite supply of imports ($\varepsilon_M = \infty$). Taking the limit of (3.25)

$$\lim_{\eta_x, \varepsilon_M \to \infty} \{\frac{\varepsilon_x(\eta_x - 1)}{(\eta_x + \varepsilon_x)} + \frac{\eta_M(1 + \varepsilon_M)}{(\eta_M + \varepsilon_M)}\} = \varepsilon_x + \eta_M > 0 \qquad (3.26)$$

Hence, a devaluation always raises net exports for a small economy.

The next condition assumes underutilised capacity at home such that increased export demand is automatically met by exports, the supply of which is infinitely elastic ($\varepsilon_x = \infty$). Moreover, there are no supply constraints abroad either, such that the supply of imports is infinitely elastic ($\eta_x = \infty$). Taking the limit of (3.25) under these assumptions

$$\lim_{\varepsilon_x, \varepsilon_M \to \infty} \{\frac{\varepsilon_x(\eta_x - 1)}{(\varepsilon_x + \eta_x)} + \frac{\eta_M(1 + \varepsilon_M)}{(\varepsilon_M + \eta_M)}\} = \eta_x + \eta_M - 1 > 0 \qquad (3.27)$$

(3.27) can be rewritten as $\eta_x + \eta_M > 1$ which is known as the Marshall–Lerner condition.

3.2.2 Limitations

As an abbreviated form of the elasticities approach, the Marshall–Lerner condition therefore suggested that a devaluation of a country's currency would improve its trade or current account balance if the sum of the price elasticities of domestic and foreign demands for imports were larger than unity. This condition therefore ensured that the increased quantity of exports following a change in relative prices after a devaluation offsets the increased cost of imports. If the condition was not met, this implied revaluation, not devaluation was necessary for restoring external balance. The key assumption of the Marshall–Lerner variant of the elasticities approach was that the supply of exports and imports were infinitely elastic. Though the macroeconomic implications of changes in export and import volumes were not considered by the approach, implicitly the assumptions about supply elasticities were only applicable to recessed economies. Hence, in this regard, the approach was inconsistent with the full employment assumption of the classical approach, yet, later on, proved to be fully compatible with open economy extensions of Keynesian macroeconomic models.

Many empirical studies subsequently sought to estimate demand elasticities based on this approach to the trade balance. Early studies suggested elasticities were low in the short run which generated 'elasticity pessimism' about trade account adjustment. Later studies also estimated the weak response of trade flows in the first year after an exchange rate change, although over longer periods estimates for industrial countries show the Marshall-Lerner condition was usually satisfied.[1]

The evidence that short run export and import demand elasticities are low also provides a justification for the so-called J-curve phenomenon, which suggests that after a devaluation or depreciation, a pre-existing trade account initially widens before eventually narrowing. J-curves can also be explained with reference to trade contracts. For instance, soon after a devaluation, recorded export and import volumes may for some months simply reflect purchasing decisions based on the old exchange rate, so that the depreciation only raises the value of recorded imports, whereas exports measured in domestic currency do not change. Moreover, sluggish trade account adjustment to changes in competitiveness may reflect lags in producing additional exports, although acknowledging supply constraints on the export side contravenes one of the assumptions underlying the Marshall–Lerner condition.

3.3   The dependent economy approach

The elasticities approach to the external accounts with its sole emphasis on the effects of relative price changes on the trade balance, to the neglect of other macroeconomic influences, obviously seemed incomplete by the 1950s, by which time Keynes' *General Theory of Employment, Interest and Money* (1936) had profoundly influenced macroeconomic thinking. On the issue of external account determination, *The General Theory* was silent. Indeed, this book can be criticised for leading modern macroeconomics astray insofar as it reasoned on the assumption of a closed economy, a line of enquiry at odds with the emphasis on international linkages in the writings of the other great English economists including David Ricardo, John Stuart Mill and Alfred Marshall.

It was left to another English economist James Meade (1951, 1952) to cast balance of payments analysis in an explicit macroeconomic framework which made sense under the rules governing the Bretton Woods system. Using a framework which was in many ways a precursor to the Mundell–Fleming approach outlined later in the book, Meade allowed for some capital mobility in his analysis of the external accounts and was first to draw the distinction between the often conflicting goals of internal balance (full employment) and external balance (balance of payments stability). At the same time, Alexander (1952) at the International Monetary Fund, highlighted the distinction between national product and national expenditure or absorption as earlier discussed in Chapter 2 and expressed in equation (1.1).

Alexander's absorption approach provided a crucial insight by stressing the importance of analysing the external accounts in the context of overall spending and production in contrast to the strictly partial nature of the elasticities approach. Alexander (1959) later attempted a synthesis of the elasticities and absorption approaches, but this was disappointing as it did not simultaneously consider the interaction of relative price and income effects.

3.3.1   The basic model

An absorption-related approach which did successfully model the contemporaneous effects of changing relative prices and expenditure was proposed by Swan (1960) and Salter (1959). What distinguished this approach was a markedly different specification of goods markets for small open economies. Previous macroeconomic approaches had often assumed implicitly that all goods were potentially exportable and that the prices of goods produced domestically were endogenous, whereas the prices of imports in foreign exchange were exogenous.

In contrast, the Swan–Salter approach highlighted the goods market dichotomy between tradables and non-tradables.[2] According to Swan, the prices a small economy receives for exports and pays for imports 'are independent of domestic conditions of supply and demand' (1960, p. 53), whereas Salter (1959) termed non-tradables as goods 'which do not enter into world trade; their prices are determined solely by internal costs and demand' (p. 226).

Also known as the 'dependent economy' or Australian model, this approach assumes a given terms of trade, here measured by the ratio of the exogenously determined prices received for exportables to the exogenously determined prices paid for importables. With this assumption, exportables and importables can be lumped together as tradables by virtue of Hicks' (1946) composite commodity theorem:

> A collection of physical things can always be treated as if they were identical in the units of a simple commodity so long as their relative prices can be assumed unchanged.
>
> (Hicks, 1946, p. 33)

Hence tradables consist of exports, imports, export substitutes and import competing goods, whereas non-tradables are usually imagined as the bulk of services or goods prevented from entering into world trade because of prohibitive transport costs or tariffs.

The centrally managed nominal exchange rate converts the given world prices of tradables into domestic currency terms ($P_T = eP_T^*$) and the real exchange rate (V), or competitiveness, is here defined as the ratio of the domestic price of non-tradables (P_N) to the price of tradables (P_T): $V \equiv P_N/P_T$.

In the dependent economy model, external balance is synonymous with a balanced trade account and capital flows are absent. Moreover, without servicing costs on earlier capital flows, the current account equates with the trade account, ignoring other international transfers. Internal balance is the correspondence between the output of, and expenditure on, non-tradables. The Salter diagram in Figure 3.1 depicts the simultaneous attainment of internal and external balance at point *E*. The production transformation curve indicates possible output combinations for existing technology and factor endowments. For a given set of production possibilities, a rise in tradable output requires forgone non-tradable output. On the other hand, the community indifference curve represents ex ante absorption in Alexander's sense.

With reference to the Figure 3.1, full equilibrium implies *OT* tradables are supplied and demanded at the given real exchange rate ensuring external balance, whereas *ON* non-tradables are supplied and demanded at the same real exchange rate ensuring internal balance.

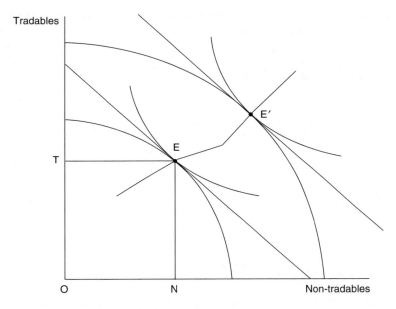

Figure 3.1 The dependent economy model

The approach suggests that departures from internal or external imbalance may occur if competitiveness changes or a disparity arises between output and expenditure. In such circumstances, a policy response simultaneously combining managed exchange rate changes and changes in autonomous expenditure becomes necessary. There are two instruments for two targets consistent with Tinbergen's (1952) rule.

For given technology and factor endowments, the supply side of the model may be expressed in symbols as $Y_{T,N} = Y_{T,N}(V)$. The expenditure side is $A_{T,N} = A_{T,N}(V, A)$ where A includes autonomous expenditure which can be influenced by fiscal or monetary policy. Hence, production of tradables and non-tradables is in the short run, simply a function of competitiveness, yet absorption is a function of both competitiveness and autonomous expenditure.

Internal balance obtains when $Y_N(V) = A_N(V, A)$ and external balance obtains when $Y_T(V) = A_T(V, A)$. Differentiating these equations totally then allows us to derive the internal and external balance loci. Starting with the internal balance locus (*NN*)

$$\frac{\partial Y_N}{\partial V} dV = \frac{\partial A_N}{\partial V} dV + \frac{\partial A_N}{\partial A} dA$$

$$\therefore \frac{dV}{dA} = \frac{\partial A_N}{\partial A} / (\frac{\partial Y_N}{\partial V} - \frac{\partial A_N}{\partial V}) > 0$$

For the external balance locus (*TT*)

$$\frac{\partial Y_T}{\partial V} dV = \frac{\partial A_T}{\partial V} dV + \frac{\partial A_T}{\partial \bar{A}} dA$$

$$\therefore \frac{dV}{dA} = \frac{\partial A_T}{\partial A} / (\frac{\partial Y_T}{\partial V} - \frac{\partial A_T}{\partial V}) < 0$$

Depicting these loci in *V–A* space yields the Swan diagram with its four 'zones of economic unhappiness' (Figure 3.2).

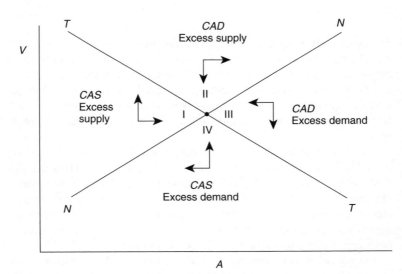

Figure 3.2   The Swan diagram

Intuitively, the internal balance schedule slopes upward because as competitiveness worsens (a rise in *V*), net exports fall, and expenditure must increase to compensate for this. The external balance schedule slopes downward because an increase in expenditure worsens net exports unless offset by an improvement in competitiveness (a fall in *V*).

Above the *NN* locus the economy has underutilised resources, below it there are excess demand pressures. Above the *TT* line the economy experiences a trade (current) account deficit, below it a trade account surplus.

An economy out of equilibrium reaches simultaneous internal and external balance through the combined use of managed exchange rate changes to alter competitiveness and activist fiscal and monetary policy to raise or lower total expenditure. For instance, an economy experiencing excess aggregate demand pressures and an external deficit (zone III) could restore internal balance by contractionary policy and restore external balance by devaluing the exchange rate.

Given its particular goods-market specification, devaluation improves the trade balance and revaluation worsens the trade balance unambiguously. Totally differentiating the expression for the trade balance in foreign exchange terms, $T^* = (Y_T(V) - A_T(V))P_T^*$ with respect to *V*, where Y_T and A_T are volumes, yields

$$dT^* = P_T^* \frac{\partial Y_T}{\partial V} dV - P_T^* \frac{\partial A_T}{\partial V} dV$$

$$\therefore \frac{dT^*}{dV} = P_T^* (\frac{\partial Y_T}{\partial V} - \frac{\partial A_T}{\partial V}) < 0$$

This result is compatible with the elasticities condition pertaining to a small country, as shown earlier, but contrasts with the conditionality of the normal Marshall–Lerner condition. Intuitively, devaluation lowers the relative price of non-traded goods to traded goods, encouraging production and discouraging absorption of tradables.

3.3.2 Limitations

Consistent with the international economic environment of the 1950s and 1960s, the original dependent economy model assumed the exchange rate was managed and ignored external capital flows and the possibility that domestic saving and investment could diverge. Once the exchange rate is permitted to float, however, external balance is automatically achieved in the model as exports must always equal imports as an equilibrium condition in the foreign exchange market. Hence, a dependent economy always finds itself on the *TT* locus of the Swan diagram and the goal of external balance becomes redundant. Unfortunately, the model cannot be so easily adapted to allow for international capital mobility, a factor which severely limits the model's usefulness as a framework for analysing external account determination in the 1990s.

3.4   Monetary approaches

The developments in international macroeconomics and balance of payments theory from the elasticities approach, which first emerged in the 1920s, to the absorption related approaches of the 1950s and 1960s mainly emphasized adjustment in the goods markets with the trade balance providing the measure of external disequilibrium. However, a different approach to the external accounts reemphasising the role of money in the external adjustment process emerged in the literature by the late 1960s and 1970s, although an earlier version of the approach had been proposed by Polak (1957), another International Monetary Fund economist (see also IMF (1977)). This approach became known as the monetary approach to the balance of payments (MABP).[3]

The MABP had more in common with the original Humean approach than other subsequent macroeconomic approaches because it restored the notion that the external adjustment process was essentially self equilibrating and not of itself a concern. Moreover, like the classical approach, it afforded the demand and supply of money balances a central role. Other Humean features of this approach were that growth in national income was exogenously determined by real factors such as advances in technology and population growth and that demands for particular national currencies by domestic residents were stable functions of a few variables, the most important being real income. Unlike the original price-specie-flow mechanism however, changes in relative export and import prices on which the elasticities approach focussed were eliminated from the analysis.

Instead of examining the trade or current account imbalance *per se*, the MABP shifted attention to the overall balance of payments as a monetary phenomenon reflecting the change in the central banks reserve holdings. With reference to our real and financial flows matrix of Chapter 2 (Figure 2.4), the analysis centred on the relationships between the money base and changes in foreign currency reserves (rows 2 and 7), with the central bank (column 5) playing a prominent role.

Another distinguishing feature of the MABP was its emphasis on stocks, in contrast to the earlier flow oriented approaches. It stressed that the flow of international reserves, as the measure of external imbalance under fixed rates, essentially reflected domestic money market disequilibrium which could only be restored when the stock demand and stock supply of real balances reached their desired levels.

3.4.1 The basic model

The monetary approach actually encompasses a wide class of models. For instance, one version of the monetary approach proposed by Dornbusch (1973) assumes a small open economy facing world prices for all goods produced and consumed, but there is no capital account. This version also invokes the output-absorption distinction. The main features of the approach are now outlined below.

The demand for (L) money is considered a stable function of income such that

$$L - kP\overline{Y} \tag{3.28}$$

where k is a parameter, P is the domestic price level and $\overline{Y}$ is constant real output at the level of full employment.

If money, simply defined as money base, is the only asset, then the difference between output and expenditure, the trade imbalance, must be equal to the change in the money base held by the public:

$$dM^S = P\overline{Y} - A \tag{3.29}$$

Furthermore, under fixed rates,

$$dR = dM^s \tag{3.30}$$

The difference between absorption and income is also related to the difference between actual and desired money holdings,

$$P\overline{Y} - A = \alpha(L - M^S)$$

$0 < \alpha < 1$, where α is an adjustment parameter. From (3.28), (3.29) and (3.30) we can write

$$dR = \alpha(kP\overline{Y} - M^S) \qquad (3.31)$$

Equation (3.31) expresses the self-correcting nature of any discrepancy between money supply and money demand. For instance, if money demand exceeds the available supply, dR will be positive, indicating that a balance of payments surplus will eventuate and persist until it raises the money supply to the level consistent with desired money holdings. On the contrary, if the domestic supply of money available to be held by residents exceeds the level desired, there will be a balance of payments deficit which will only last until desired and actual money stocks are again equal. Graphically, the model can be illustrated by a simple phase diagram (Figure 3.3) which shows that the adjustment mechanism is stable.

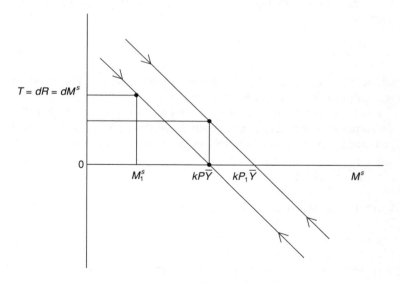

Figure 3.3   The monetary approach to the balance of payments

If for instance the money supply is M_1^S which falls short of desired cash holdings at $kP\overline{Y}$ then there would be reduced absorption (or hoarding) by domestic residents in an attempt to accumulate cash balances. This would manifest as a trade surplus matched by a rise in reserves. A steady expansion of the domestic money supply continues until desired and actual money stocks again coincide. At that point external balance is restored.

Several important policy implications followed from the MABP. First, the approach stressed, as did Hume, that under fixed rates the money supply is in the long run endogenous, determined not by the central bank but essentially by the public's demand for cash balances. Furthermore, devaluations will only have a transitory effect on the balance of payments and only to the extent that they affect stock equilibrium in the money market. This is also shown in the figure above. By invoking the absolute purchasing power parity condition ($P = eP^*$) devaluation firstly raises the domestic price level to P_1. Domestic residents again attempt to restore real cash balances to the previous level by reducing absorption. In so doing, a balance of payments surplus arises and persists until the nominal money supply increases (proportionate to the increase in the price level) to restore money stock equilibrium.

Note that the nature of the mechanism transmitting the change in the exchange rate to the balance on the external account are altogether different from the elasticities approach. Indeed, advocates of the MABP considered the elasticities conditions irrelevant since all prices inevitably rose in the devaluing country to the extent of the devaluation itself.

3.4.2 Limitations and extensions

The MABP was in some respects a restatement of the original classical approach. Similarly, it is subject to criticism about its implicit assumption of free and flexible labour and goods markets. With the generalized move to floating rates in the 1970s, the MABP became somewhat redundant as a means of understanding the external accounts; with floating exchange rates, the overall balance of payments as a measure of a central bank's support for a particular exchange rate ceased to be the constraint it had been hitherto under the Bretton Woods system.

Accordingly, attention shifted to the determinants of the exchange rate as the macroeconomic variable reflecting the pressure of external adjustment. The essential ingredients of the MABP were then deployed to model exchange rate determination with continued emphasis on the role played by relative money demands and supplies. Implicitly, however, these models accepted that the traditional notion of external imbalance as a quantity constraint no longer mattered for policy purposes.

Relatedly, the portfolio balance (PB) approach to the open economy developed from the 1960s and included domestic and foreign bonds in addition to money.[4] It extended earlier work on general portfolio theory advanced by Markowitz (1952) and Tobin (1958). The PB approach usually suggests capital flows are short-lived phenomena which cease once desired and actual financial asset holdings equate. Financial capital is not perfectly mobile by assumption, though alternative financial assets remain gross substitutes in demand. By restricting attention to nominal financial wealth held by domestic residents and by using total financial wealth as a scale variable in asset demand equations, the PB approach has been used to explain the short run comparative static effects of changes in the domestic supply of money and bonds on the nominal exchange rate and domestic interest rate.

Within the PB class of open economy models, some authors have recognized a role for the current account in terms of its implications for the international investment position and hence for financial wealth holdings. For example, some authors have explicitly modelled the feedback effects of current account imbalances on the exchange rate.[5] However, the emphasis in these models is on financial phenomena to the neglect of real phenomena.

4
Intertemporal Trade, Capital Mobility and Interest Rates

This chapter analyses the relationship between international finance and macroeconomic activity by combining aspects of production, trade and finance theory. It adapts and extends the precepts of Irving Fisher's (1930) intertemporal theory of interest rates by first highlighting the linkages between consumption, saving, investment, international financial flows, interest rates, national income, foreign debt and national wealth. It then shows how international trade in saving confers macroeconomic welfare gains before reconciling intertemporal analysis with a loanable funds approach that can be used as a basis for interpreting international capital mobility.

4.1 The intertemporal approach

In a two-sector economy, comprised of households and firms, it can be assumed that aggregate output and expenditure are determined separately as suggested by absorption related approaches to external adjustment. Firms invest and combine labour, land, existing capital with given technology to produce maximum output over two periods of time (the present and the whole of the future), whereas households have preferences for present consumption (C_1) versus future consumption (C_2) and supply labour inelastically. Once again, the analysis abstracts from capital stock depreciation.

Central to the intertemporal approach is the notion of an investment opportunities function (f) which transforms forgone present consumption (saving) into future output (Y_2) through additional capital accumulation (investment I_1). The transformation curve is defined as $F(Y_1, Y_2) = 0$ and the intertemporal production function is of the form $Y_2 = Y_1(K, L) + f(I_1)$. To fix ideas about the intertemporal approach, first consider some basic optimising conditions, initially in the closed economy context. These conditions form the basis for subsequent diagrammatic analysis for the open economy.

The economy's problem is to maximise its consumption or living standards (l) intertemporally, given present output and the available investment opportunities. The economy's utility function is therefore l (C_1, C_2). The present values of the future stream of output (Y_2) and consumption (C_2) are $\dfrac{Y_2}{1+r}$ *and* $\dfrac{C_2}{1+r}$ where r is the prevailing domestic interest rate. Output produced by firms over both periods, $F(Y_1, Y_2)$, is maximised and the solvency condition for households is that income received over both periods is sufficient to cover intertemporal consumption. That is

$$Y_1 + \frac{Y_2}{1+r} = C_1 + \frac{C_2}{1+r} \tag{4.1}$$

Hence if all of output produced by firms is consumed by households over the two periods, the problem becomes maximise the Lagrangean L (C, Y, λ):

$$L(C_1, C_2, Y_1, Y_2, \lambda_1, \lambda_2) = l(C_1, C_2) + \lambda_1 \left(Y_1 + \left[\frac{Y_2}{1+r} \right] - C_1 - \left[\frac{C_2}{1+r} \right] \right)$$
$$+ \lambda_2 F(Y_1, Y_2) \tag{4.2}$$

Then the first-order conditions state

$$D_1 L = D_1 l - \lambda_1 = 0 \tag{4.3}$$

$$D_2 L = D_2 l - \left(\frac{1}{1+r} \right) \lambda_1 = 0 \tag{4.4}$$

$$D_3 L = \lambda_1 + \lambda_2 D_1 F = 0 \tag{4.5}$$

$$D_4 L = \left(\frac{1}{1+r} \right) \lambda_1 + \lambda_2 D_2 F = 0 \tag{4.6}$$

$$D_5 L = Y_1 + \left(\frac{Y_2}{1+r} \right) - C_1 - \left(\frac{C_2}{1+r} \right) = 0 \tag{4.7}$$

$$D_6L = F(Y_1, Y_2) = 0 \tag{4.8}$$

From (4.3) and (4.4) it follows that for households

$$MRS = \frac{D_1 l}{D_2 l} = 1 + r \tag{4.9}$$

and for firms from (4.5) and (4.6)

$$MRT = \frac{D_1 F}{D_2 F} = 1 + r \tag{4.10}$$

Hence, $MRS = MRT$ or the marginal rate of substitution of present for future consumption equals the marginal rate of transformation of present into future income.

4.1.1 Graphical analysis

With these results as a basis, it is possible to depict the welfare gains from international trade in saving using a Fisherian framework.[1] In Figure 4.1, if present period saving is zero, then in a certain world with unchanged production technology, output 'endowed' in the future would be the same as in the present (as conveyed by the 45° line). With positive saving, however, the productive investment which abstinence allows yields higher future output and hence income, as determined by the investment opportunities frontier capturing domestic firms' ability to transform current income into future income. The marginal productivity of capital declines when more domestic capital is combined with the available supply of other resource inputs.

If capital is immobile internationally, the equilibrium return on capital for the economy would be determined by the intersection of investment opportunities and households' saving propensities. Hence, in equilibrium both the economy-wide return on capital and households' rate of time preference would equal the real interest rate. The slope of the investment opportunities curve and the consumption indifference curve would be $1 + r$ at the point of tangency. Therefore, if nations' capital markets are isolated, the range of international interest rates would reflect the diversity of national saving propensities and investment opportunities.

However, with a move from zero capital mobility to full capital mobility, the correspondence between aggregate domestic saving and

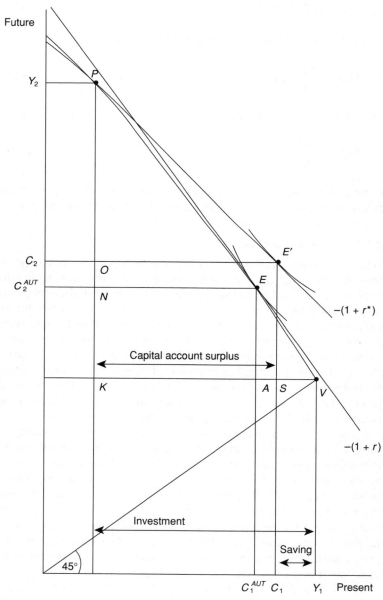

Figure 4.1   Intertemporal gains from foreign investment (a)

investment would be broken. The Fisher separation theorem, which suggests that financial markets enable consumption and investment decisions to be made independently, would therefore hold in an international macroeconomic setting. Moreover, in the absence of uncertainty, and abstracting from the complication of changing exchange rate expectations, domestic and foreign claims to real capital would become perfect substitutes. Through arbitrage, a small country's interest rate should equate with the prevailing world interest rate such that capital becomes perfectly mobile. There are other measures of capital mobility, however, and the complete set of these conditions will be fully defined shortly.

Figure 4.1 also illustrates the macroeconomic benefits of full capital mobility over zero mobility. If the autarky interest rate is initially higher than the world interest rate (r^*), full capital mobility necessarily creates a saving-investment imbalance, thus generating a *KAS* for the financially open economy. With reference to the figure, domestic capital formation rises by distance *KS* since investment continues up to the point where the rate of return on capital equals the foreign interest rate.

The exact response of present consumption to interest rate changes is, however, a matter of some theoretical controversy. A fall in the interest rate makes current consumption less expensive relative to future consumption, discouraging saving – the substitution effect. On the other hand, the reduced income from interest receipts encourages households to save more – the income effect. Pre-Keynesian economists assumed the dominance of the substitution effect making current saving a rising function of the interest rate, but in theory this ambiguity cannot be resolved as Bailey (1957) demonstrated.

Assuming the dominance of the substitution effect, saving falls by distance *AS*, with point *E* to the north-east of the initial consumption point. If, however, the income effect dominated, the new consumption point would lie north-west. In the case where the substitution and income effects offset, the new equilibrium would lie directly above the old. Foreign investment in the small country is matched by a collective *CAS* run by the rest of the world and is equivalent to distance *KA* in the first period, the difference between domestic saving (*AV*) and domestic investment (*KV*).

Under the lower world interest rate regime, the equilibrium optimising condition is

$$MRS = MRT = 1 + r^* \tag{4.11}$$

Income and consumption both today and tomorrow can be higher than under zero capital mobility, again affirming that foreign investment under full capital mobility improves the economy's standard of living. Provided initial expectations about the income producing potential of capital are fulfilled, future income will always be adequate to repay the external financial liabilities run up to finance the higher domestic capital accumulation. This is because, geometrically, distance *OP* in Figure 4.1 will exceed distance *OE* as long as the interest rate is positive, since the slope of the budget line must then exceed unity. That is

$$\frac{OP}{OE} = 1 + r^* > 1 \tag{4.12}$$

The process of real capital transfer associated with the foreign investment recorded on the financial account is matched on the current account by either imported investment goods or imported consumption goods which release resources for domestic capital production. Since introducing intermediate goods would considerably complicate the analysis, it has been implicitly assumed throughout that all goods are final goods.

It is also possible to adapt the analysis to the two region case, whereby interest rates become endogenously determined. Figure 4.2 shows the effects of integrating the capital markets of two previously autarkic regions with different investment opportunities and saving propensities. After allowing unrestricted foreign investment, arbitrage again ensures a single interest rate. Country *A*'s initial interest rate falls and country *B*'s rises. Living standards rise in both countries and the equilibrium condition is that

$$MRS^A = MRS^B = MRT^A = MRT^B = 1 + r\,' \tag{4.13}$$

The external account triangles suggest that a move to full capital mobility from zero mobility creates capital inflow or a *CAD* of *FG* in country *A* matched by capital outflow or a *CAS* of *IJ* in *B*. To repay its international obligations in the future, economy *A* transfers *EF* income to *B*. Unambiguously, foreign investment under full capital mobility raises living standards in both regions because the trade in saving

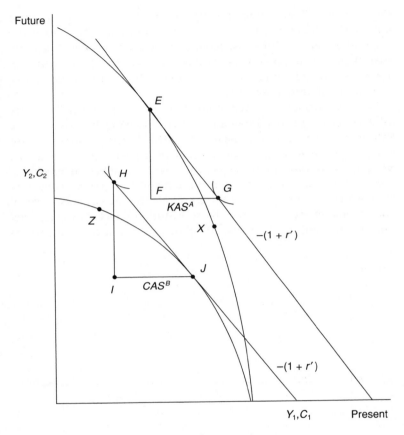

Figure 4.2   Intertemporal gains from foreign investment (b)

allows households to reach higher levels of welfare compared with those possible in isolation; that is, for country A, $G > X$ and for country B, $H > Z$.

4.1.2   Offer curve analysis

The intertemporal approach to foreign investment provides a basis for introducing offer curves, usually only employed in the pure theory of international merchandise trade, to model the external accounts. Casting the intertemporal approach in terms of offer curves serves to highlight that, contrary to the approaches to the external accounts outlined in Chapter 3, international trade in saving determines the external accounts with consequent real effects. It also demonstrates that there are important similarities between the pure theory of international trade and the determination of the external accounts in a general equilibrium framework.

Figure 4.3 depicts an intertemporal offer curve for a small country which opens itself up to international trade in saving. It is based on the information contained in Figure 4.1. The horizontal axis records inward foreign investment or the present period *CAD*, whereas the vertical axis records the subsequent KAS which will be generated.

Here it is assumed that the substitution effect on present consumption of an interest rate change at least offsets any income effect. Even if the income effect dominated the substitution effect, however, offer curves can still be constructed, provided the extra investment

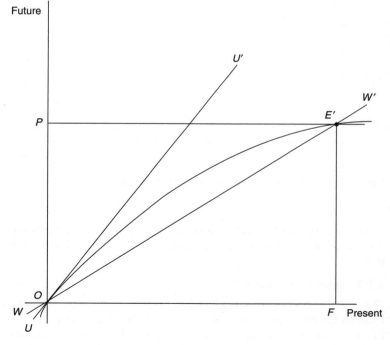

Figure 4.3   Intertemporal offer curve (a)

stemming from the lower interest rate exceeds any additional consumption in the first period.

The line *UU'* has the same slope in absolute value terms as the autarky budget line in Figure 4.1. Foreign investment continues to rise as the domestic interest rate approaches the world rate. When the domestic interest rate equals the world rate as shown by line *WW'*, the small country imports *OF* of foreign saving in period one, which it later repays with interest as *OP*. The triangle *E'OP* is the same as the intertemporal trade triangle *E'OP* in Figure 4.1.

For the two region case, the general equilibrium outcome is as shown in Figure 4.4. The intersecting ray must lie above the 45° line, whose slope equals unity, if the interest rate is to be positive.

In parallel with orthodox international trade theory, the offer curves demonstrate that when foreign investment is allowed and capital markets are fully integrated, a common price, the return on capital,

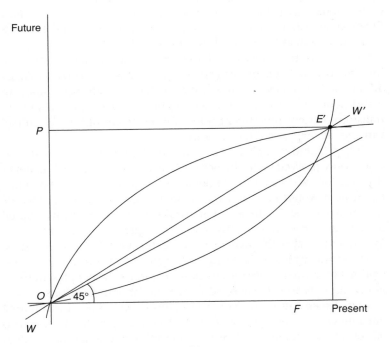

Figure 4.4 Intertemporal offer curve (b)

must prevail, and this price clears the unified markets. Foreign investment confers welfare gains if economies' real interest rates would be different without trade. Economies would not engage in intertemporal trade, however, irrespective of the extent of capital mobility, if domestic interest rates were identical in autarky.

4.1.3   Capital market integration, foreign debt and wealth

As outlined in Chapter 1, the abolition of official restrictions governing cross border transactions over recent decades has transformed the financial markets of many economies from being heavily regulated and segmented, into ones that are lightly regulated and more internationally integrated. Access to international financial capital and services has increased greatly which has boosted borrowing and lending opportunities and enhanced capital mobility. Whereas much of the foregoing analysis focused on international flow magnitudes, this section shifts attention to aggregate stocks to model the stock adjustment effects of international financial liberalisation. In particular, it shows how financial globalisation may affect a nation's external indebtedness position, as well as the value of its capital stock and wealth.

To illustrate the effect of international financial liberalisation on investment, foreign debt, the capital stock and wealth consider Figure 4.5 below. The analysis is initially restricted to firms' behaviour. An investment opportunities frontier again captures firms' ability to transform current investment into a future stream of income and all variables are expressed in real terms.

With prohibitive exchange controls in place, domestic investment would only proceed up to the point where the return on capital, net of depreciation, was equal to the domestic interest rate, r. In the figure, investment would be K and the present value of the future income stream would be W. In a certain world with a competitive capital market and no transactions costs, the present value of firms' investment is also the market value of the firms' common shares, which in this simple model equals the value of the economy's assets. Optimal investment decisions by firms maximise the net present value of investments and also maximise the value of national assets.

After dispensing with exchange controls and other institutional impediments to foreign investment, it may be possible for firms to borrow at a lower rate of interest (r^*) prevailing in international capital markets.

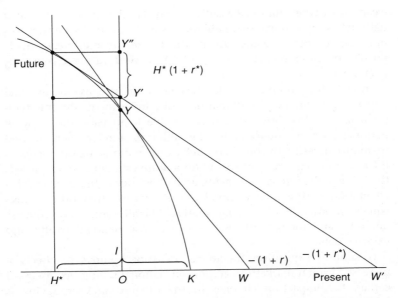

Figure 4.5 International financial liberalisation, external debt and national wealth

With reference to the Figure 4.5, domestic firms borrow H^* abroad after deregulation which then becomes a stock adjustment increase in foreign debt. By investing $K + H^* = I$, firms generate future income of Y'', the present value of which is $Y''/(1 + r^*)$ or, $H^* + W'$. However, since H^* plus $r^* H^*$ in interest must eventually be paid to foreign lenders, the future income accrual to residents shrinks to Y'. The present value of the future income stream to domestic residents, is $\dfrac{Y'' - H^*(1 + r^*)}{(1 + r^*)}$ or W'.

Hence, this approach implies that under conditions where external borrowing is freely permitted, and cheaper funds are available from somewhere abroad, an increase in external indebtedness funding additional real investment should lead to a rise in the value of national wealth, provided the increase in the present value of the capital stock, as reflected in equity prices, exceeds the increase in external indebtedness.

Put another way, the increase in external liabilities is more than offset by an increase in the market value of assets, such that national wealth rises, where national wealth is defined as the difference between national assets and external liabilities. Note from the figure that this must be so since the increase in the future income stream made possible by the external borrowing $Y'' - Y'$, exceeds future repayments, $H^*(1 + r^*)$.

Though the emphasis so far has been on the use of external borrowing to finance additional domestic investment, the intertemporal model also shows that it is possible to increase the value of national assets and hence national wealth if the foreign loans are used to finance investment abroad. In such a case, national wealth increases if the net present value of the additional investment abroad exceeds the value of the foreign borrowing used to finance it. In summary, this adaptation of the intertemporal model suggests that other things equal, international financial market liberalisation may equalise domestic and foreign interest rates and raise national wealth and external debt.

To simplify exposition, the above discussion ignored the effects of increased capital market integration on national saving. As discussed earlier, the impact of changes in the interest rates on saving is somewhat ambiguous in a theoretical sense, since there may be offsetting income and substitution effects. If the substitution and income effects of a fall in the cost of capital exactly offset each other, present saving becomes inelastic with respect to the interest rate.

Using this assumption, standard for instance in textbook discussion of closed and open economy Keynesian models where the interest rate is not an argument in the consumption function, it is possible to imagine consumption indifference curves tangential to points Y and Y'. The wealth levels OW and OW' then represent the net present value of additional future consumption stemming from additional investment.

The above model also implicitly assumes 'fundamental valuation efficiency' which according to Tobin (1984) prevails when the prices of financial claims to capital accurately reflect all future payments to which those claims give title. Many would argue, however, that 'fundamental valuation efficiency' does not always prevail, as evidenced by the phenomenon of speculative bubbles followed by sharp collapses, as occurs in stock markets from time to time. This then raises perennial and complex questions about the nature of expectations formation and financial market efficiency, and indeed the very worth of financial market activity.[2] Many of these issues remain, and perhaps will always remain, unresolved and a full discussion lies beyond the scope of this chapter. Suffice to say that we presume over longer periods, such as a decade, that the valuation of the private capital stock is at least roughly efficient, in an 'on average' sense and that financial markets are not persistently prone to waves of irrational behaviour.

Nonetheless, it is still possible to capture the effects of well founded revisions to expectations about future income streams in the above model. If, for instance, expectations were suddenly revised upwards on the basis of new information about investment prospects, the investment opportunities frontier would bow upward from the origin. Though not drawn in the figure above, it is relatively straightforward to demonstrate that under the assumptions of the approach, an upward revision of investment prospects would further increase foreign debt, investment and national net worth, provided foreign lenders concurred with the upward revisions. If they did not, a risk premium would then be added to the foreign interest rate on offer limiting the investment, capital stock and external debt increase. Risk premia and how they arise are further discussed in the next chapter.

4.2 Loanable funds approach

The intertemporal approach suggests that a country's external accounts, as a component of the larger framework of social accounts, are best perceived as a record of international capital flows between countries, rather than as the difference between exports and imports of goods and services. The intertemporal approach explicitly recognises that with capital mobility, the external accounts are a nation's saving-investment imbalance, consistent with the accounting flow of funds matrix of Chapter 2. So far, however liquid funds as such have not been afforded any major role in the capital centred approaches. To remedy this omission, we now introduce the loanable funds approach.

The loanable funds theory of interest rate determination advocated by Robertson (1940), amongst others, explicitly recognises financial flows in the context of saving and investment behaviour. Originally specified for a closed economy, the loanable funds approach as exposited for instance by Tsiang (1989) suggests that on the demand side of the money market, there are d^1 funds required to finance firms' investment, d^2 funds required to finance firms' replacement capital (that is, depreciation reserves), d^3 funds to be added to inactive balances held as liquid reserves (that is, hoarding), and d^4 funds required to finance households' consumption in excess of disposable income (that is, dissaving).

On the supply side, there are s^1 funds due to the excess of households' disposable income over planned consumption expenditure, s^2 depreciation reserves taken out of firms' gross sales of the preceding period, s^3 funds used from previously held inactive money balances (that is, dishoarding) and s^4 funds representing the net creation of additional money by banks. In an open economy, again consistent with our earlier flow of funds matrix (Figure 2.4), we can add s^5 funds provided by the rest of the world.

The equilibrium condition for the total demand and supply of loanable funds is then

$$d^1 + d^2 + d^3 + d^4 = s^1 + s^2 + s^3 + s^4 + s^5 \tag{4.14}$$

which can be rearranged as

$$\underbrace{}_{d^1 + d^2} \; - \; \underbrace{}_{(s^1 + s^2 - d^4 + s^4)} + \; \underbrace{\text{Net hoarding}}_{d^3 - s^3} = \underbrace{KAS}_{s^5} \tag{4.15}$$

Written this way we can see how the flow record of external imbalance relates to the demand and supply of loanable funds. Domestic and foreign money may be directly supplied by households and by non-residents to domestic firms for investment purposes via the purchase of equities and debt instruments from firms. Or excess funds may be supplied indirectly via financial intermediaries.

The loanable funds perspective also recognises hoarding activity, or changes in demand for inactive cash balances, the basis for which may be explained by the precautionary and speculative motives, first outlined by Keynes (1936). In this way, the approach provides a link to the monetary underpinnings of the Mundell-Fleming model, outlined later in Chapter 6. Though we abstract from hoarding behaviour in what follows, on the assumption that hoarding is relatively insignificant in relation to gross saving and investment flows, it is of interest to note that an increase in hoarding (dishoarding) should marginally increase (decrease) the *KAS* if the demand for investible funds exceeds the domestic supply.

Since domestic saving equals households' lending, and since domestic firms' investment equals borrowing at home and from abroad, the earlier intertemporal framework can now be entirely translated to present period analysis with reference to the demand and supply of loanable funds.

In Figure 4.6, firms' demand for funds becomes a decreasing function of the interest rate, whereas the supply of funds lent by households becomes an increasing function of the interest rate. We continue to abstract from the effects of exchange rate expectations and assume all variables are expressed in real terms. The investment possibilities frontier of the intertemporal framework suggests that domestic firms will borrow extra funds if the interest rate is less than the return on

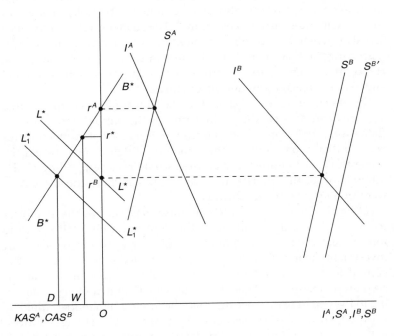

Figure 4.6 Loanable funds and foreign investment

additional real capital accumulation. The slope of the saving schedule is positive if the substitution effect dominates the income effect.

Schedule B^*B^* in the left panel shows economy A's excess demand for saving or its KAS for given interest rates with full capital mobility. If the economy is small and the foreign interest rate is r^*, the KAS is OW because the supply of foreign saving is perfectly elastic at any rate below r^A, the autarky interest rate. A fall in the world interest rate would, ceteris paribus, therefore raise the small country's KAS. In the two region case, schedule L^*L^* is introduced to show B's excess supply of saving (CAS) for interest rates above r^B, B's autarky interest rate.

This framework may now be used to predict the impact on the external accounts of various exogenous shocks. If, for instance, a decrease in time preference abroad raises foreign saving, the L^*L^* schedule would shift down to $L_1^* L_1^*$, lowering the equilibrium interest rate for both countries. A's KAS rises to OD to match B's KAD. Similarly, it can be shown quite easily that a fall in the demand for investible funds in B has the same effect. Hence, with unrestricted foreign investment, A's KAB can also be determined entirely by changes in investment and saving behaviour in B. The shared external imbalance can also change due to shifts in the L^*L^* schedule which shifts down narrowing the KAS when either A's investment falls or its saving rises. Hence, the extent of foreign investment depends on either internal and external macroeconomic disturbances.

The effects of increased capital market integration on the external accounts can also be shown in terms of the simple flow of funds framework. For instance, with reference to Figure 4.7, if capital controls were initially prohibitive, the domestic interest rate would be domestically determined at real interest rate r, corresponding to the intersection of the interest inelastic saving schedule, and the downward sloping investment schedule.

Following deregulation which permits foreign borrowing at a lower real interest rate, the domestic real interest rate would fall to r^*, the foreign real interest rate. Simultaneously, there would be a rise in investment financed by foreigners, and hence a rise of AC in the current account deficit. If capital was initially only partially mobile, on account of quantitative capital controls which limited foreign borrowing to the extent of distance AB, then the interest differential would be $r' - r^*$ which should disappear after the abolition of exchange controls. If the nation was initially a net debtor, saving would be defined as

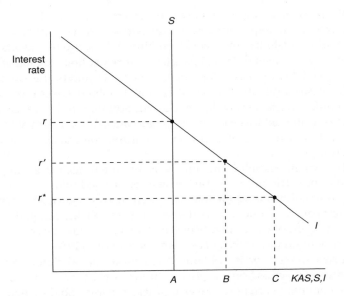

Figure 4.7 Capital market integration and the external accounts

domestic saving, that is, net of interest payments paid on previously accumulated external debt. It also follows the wider is the initial interest differential, the lower is the correspondence between domestic saving and investment at a given level of income.

4.3 Further defining capital mobility

The preceding analysis has shown that international financial flows can unambiguously raise a nation's standard of living when compared to zero capital mobility where capital mobility was characterised by the international equalisation of interest rates. But how is international capital mobility actually measured and to what extent has international financial liberalisation enhanced it?

When considering the extent of international capital market integration, an important distinction is that between international asset substitutability and capital mobility.[3] If economic agents are indifferent between holding financial securities at home or abroad for given yield differentials and exchange rate expectations, the assets are perfectly substitutable. The extent of capital mobility governs whether economic agents may achieve desired portfolio holdings and in practice is limited by factors such as ignorance of foreign investment opportunities and the phenomena of country, political and exchange rate risk.

The extent of capital mobility may be tested against a range of conditions.[4] The most comprehensive set of conditions for gauging capital mobility would include (1) closed interest parity, (2) covered interest parity, (3) uncovered interest parity, (4) real interest parity and (5) the extent of correlation between changes in domestic saving and investment (as proposed by Feldstein and Horioka (1980)).

Closed interest parity obtains if financial capital flows equalise interest rates across borders when debt instruments are denominated in a common currency. Covered interest parity holds when the difference between the forward and spot exchange rates entirely reflects interest differentials on debt instruments denominated in different currencies. If covered interest parity does not hold, this suggests there are unexploited profit opportunities from interest arbitrage. Assuming arbitrage, the above equality will only fail to hold exactly if there is uninsurable risk, large transactions costs or exchange controls.

Uncovered interest parity (UIP) holds when capital flows equalise expected rates of return on bonds denominated in different currencies, after allowing for exchange rate expectations. It may be expressed as

$$i - i^* = \hat{E} \qquad\qquad (4.16)$$

where $\hat{E}$ is anticipated currency depreciation, i is the domestic nominal interest rate and i^* the foreign nominal interest rate. For UIP to hold empirically *ex post*, we must assume that agents are risk neutral and that observed nominal interest rates incorporate a premium for (rationally) expected future exchange rate movements. Alternative forms of UIP assuming, say, adaptive expectations could conceivably hold ex ante, though most specifications jointly propose risk neutrality and rational expectations in testing the relationship.

Real interest parity is simply the equalisation of real interest rates:

$$r = r^* \tag{4.17}$$

For real interest parity to hold, however, both UIP and purchasing power parity (PPP) must hold. A simple proof of this is as follows. Since real *ex ante* interest rates at home and abroad are $r = i^* - \pi$ and $r^* = i^* - \pi^*$ (where π and π^* are the expected inflation rates at home and abroad), it follows that the real interest differential is

$$r - r^* = i - i^* - \pi + \pi^* \tag{4.18}$$

Since the UIP condition is $i - i^* = \hat{E}$ and *ex ante* PPP is simply $\pi - \pi^* = \hat{E}$, both UIP and PPP must hold exactly and at all times to equalise real interest rates internationally. These conditions are furthered considered in the next chapter.

Another test of capital mobility ascribed to Feldstein and Horioka (1980) adopts a quite different perspective to the above conditions, which test capital mobility by measuring returns on debt instruments. The Feldstein–Horioka (FH) interpretation of capital mobility focuses on aggregate investment-saving imbalances and suggests that if international capital markets are highly integrated then there is likely to be little correlation between increases in the level of saving in one particular country and that country's level of investment.

Another way of putting this is that in an open economy, saving and investment behaviour should be independent of each other in the spirit of the Fisher separation theorem. If saving is free to move internationally, it will be used to finance additional investment around the globe with little used to finance extra investment at home. The FH proposition has been perceived as an alternative measure of capital mobility and has spawned an extensive empirical literature.

In their original paper, Feldstein and Horioka empirically tested an equation for OECD economies of the form

$$I/Y = a + bS/Y + \varepsilon \tag{4.19}$$

where a and b are coefficients, ε is a stochastic error term and the other nominal variables are as earlier defined. In short, they suggested b

should be zero if capital was perfectly mobile. However, Feldstein and Horioka's evidence of a high correlation between domestic saving and investment levels for OECD countries implied a low level of international capital mobility with results showing that domestic saving passed into domestic investment (the 'savings retention coefficient') almost one to one.

The FH approach to measuring capital mobility was subsequently criticised by several authors. For instance, some claimed that, to minimize divergences between domestic saving and investment, governments tended to automatically react to current account imbalances through fiscal responses, by changing public saving and investment to offset external account imbalances. This 'policy-reaction' argument is the 'twin deficits' hypothesis in another guise.

More recent studies have addressed many of the theoretical and empirical criticisms levelled against the original FH methodology and found that although the savings retention coefficient had fallen for OECD countries, it was still higher than would be expected in a world of high capital mobility. High saving–investment correlations cannot, however, be interpreted in isolation as evidence of imperfect capital mobility, since the FH definition of capital mobility only holds if real interest parity holds and the real interest rate is determined exogenously to the country in question.

To demonstrate why the interest parity conditions and the small country assumption are necessary and sufficient for the FH condition, consider Figure 4.8. Assume a small economy is initially in equilibrium, saving equals investment and all of the parity conditions outlined above are fulfilled, so that $r = r^*$. According to the FH proposition, perfect capital mobility would obtain if, following an increase in domestic saving, foreign outward investment increases by distance a, as manifested in an inflation-adjusted *CAS*. However, for this to occur all other conditions for capital mobility must be fulfilled since the domestic interest rate must still equal the foreign rate.

Alternatively, if capital is completely immobile according to the FH proposition, the additional saving generates increased investment at home and instead of capital outflow, the domestic interest rate falls below the world rate. In light of the above analysis macroeconomic welfare is maximised if a *CAS* is generated, but is suboptimal if immobility prevails and the interest differential widens.

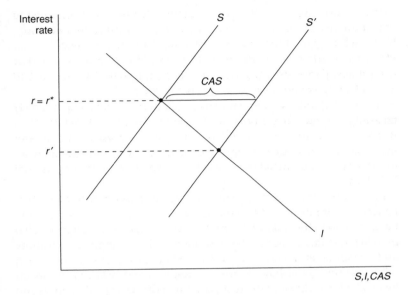

Figure 4.8 Interest parity and the FH condition

4.3.1 Empirical evidence

The empirical evidence on capital mobility in the wake of financial market liberalisation suggests that capital mobility increased in OECD countries during the 1980s and was indeed highly mobile if judged against some of the above capital mobility criteria.

For instance, on the basis of the closed interest parity condition, interest differentials on Eurocurrency borrowings had largely disappeared for the major OECD countries by the mid-1980s. There is also strong evidence in favour of covered interest parity holding for the major currencies. On the contrary, the international evidence does not support uncovered interest parity. This failure of UIP empirically can perhaps be explained with reference to time-varying risk premia and irrationally formed expectations about exchange rate movements, the determination of which is not completely under-stood. It is also plausible that exchange rate uncertainty has increased during the floating era, characterised as it is by such wide nominal exchange rate fluctuations.

Tests of real interest parity reveal that there has been some narrowing of real interest differentials consistent with increased capital mobility. Nonetheless, given the failure of UIP to hold and the evidence against PPP, particularly over shorter periods, it should not be surprising that real interest parity also fails to hold exactly, for, as derived above, UIP and PPP are preconditions for real interest parity.[5]

Finally, empirical studies have suggested that, on the basis of the FH measure, capital mobility has increased. Further evidence of a weakening of the correspondence between nations' saving and investment behaviour is simply provided by the worldwide increase in international financial flows and by the size of economies' external imbalances.

In summary, though it appears that capital mobility is still less than perfect, the empirical evidence suggests that, on balance, capital mobility has increased in the wake of international financial liberalisation. Capital mobility remains imperfect because increased exchange rate volatility under floating rates has tended to reduce financial asset substitutability; other reasons would have to include the inherent riskiness of foreign investment, the threat of the reimposition of official capital controls and remaining institutional practices which ensure part of domestic saving is directed largely toward financing strictly domestic activity, as for example with private household saving lodged with specialised financial institutions such as building societies.

Furthermore, some direct foreign investment may occur more for the purpose of overcoming goods and services trade restrictions than for strictly obtaining a higher rate of return on capital. There is also evidence that fund managers of large institutions have actively sought to diversify asset holdings internationally in order to minimise risk due to uncertain returns. Hence, in practice, consistent with standard portfolio theory, capital flows may be driven to a large extent by the expected variance of returns on capital and not just the return itself.

Though it was argued above, that the greater is capital mobility, the greater the macroeconomic welfare gains, there is a contrary view which suggests capital mobility has become 'excessive'. Tobin (1978), for instance, echoing Keynes' (1936, ch. 13) views on the inherent irrationality of financial markets, raises concerns about destabilising exchange rate movements which cause sustained deviations of real exchange rates from fundamentals with adverse implications for domestic inflation, output and employment.

As a remedy, Tobin proposed that international capital mobility be limited by throwing some 'sand on the wheels' of the international financial system; specifically, by imposing a worldwide financial transactions tax of one percent on the value of any spot conversion of one currency into another. However, it would obviously be difficult to apply such a tax consistently world wide. The proposal also ignores the macroeconomic welfare losses that could result if foreign capital, irrespective of its maturity, is prevented from flowing to areas where it earns its highest risk adjusted rate of return.

4.4 Limitations

In recent decades, greater capital mobility resulted from the increased global integration of capital markets in the wake of worldwide financial liberalisation. This has facilitated higher transnational capital flows which contributed to wider external balances. This chapter has shown that under current conditions of highly mobile financial capital there are potential gains from international trade in saving and that foreign investment has important real macroeconomic implications.

It benefits some countries to lend excess saving to others and thereby run CAS's, at the same time as it benefits others with excess investment opportunities to borrow foreign saving and run CAD's. Foreign investment or capital account surpluses can indeed be beneficial, in a macroeconomic sense, for foreign funds help a nation expand its stock of productive capital.

Like the early approaches of the previous chapter, the intertemporal model of the open economy also has limitations worth identifying. For instance, in the two-sector Fisherian approach, agents are somewhat unrealistically assumed to have perfect foresight with no role for uncertainty in the model. Yet some of the key variables in the intertemporal analysis are by nature inherently uncertain – for instance, the expected productivity of capital and hence future income streams.

The location of firms' actual investment possibilities frontier is therefore perhaps better understood as lying within a range, the size of which is determined by the extent of uncertainty. Moreover, the position of the frontier changes whenever there are supply shocks or changes in technology. Households are also usually uncertain about the future income on which they base their consumption plans. If future income happens to be less than expected, consumption may therefore prove unsustainable. Alternatively, there would be disequilibrium if income is higher than expected. The intertemporal approach also neglects public sector activity and hence does not explicitly allow for an interpretation of the effects of fiscal policy on the external accounts. However, fiscal policy can be analysed easily enough within the more general loanable funds framework. For instance, it is possible to consider the effects of fiscal changes on either the S^A or I^A schedules of earlier Figure 4.6 where these schedules now represent total domestic private and public saving and total domestic private and public investment.

If there is a fall in public saving following fiscal expansion, the S^A schedule should shift leftwards, widening the external balance, assuming full capital mobility. Similarly, a rise in public investment expenditure could shift the I^A schedule rightwards, increasing capital inflow. Other underlying assumptions of the intertemporal approach can also be questioned. For instance, prices may not adjust rapidly to clear the goods markets in the background, firms and labour unions may exercise monopoly power and there may be price signalling distortions in both goods and financial markets due to externalities. Furthermore, if international capital mobility rises in response to distortionary capital income tax measures, then macroeconomic welfare may in fact be lower, not higher as a consequence of any induced capital movements.

The intertemporal model also abstracts from the business cycle under the assumptions of market clearing and price flexibility, ensuring unemployment is at the 'natural rate' at all times. As output is essentially supply-side determined through a macroeconomic production function, the approach is sharply at odds with Keynesian inspired models which stress factors affecting aggregate demand including the fiscal and monetary policy instruments at the disposal of the authorities. While many of the above assumptions may be technically difficult to relax in the intertemporal model, any relaxation is unlikely to change the broad conclusions about the welfare benefits of capital mobility.

This approach also somewhat unrealistically underemphasized the exchange rate. Moreover, by not identifying a role for the central bank and the money supply, it failed to account for the impact of domestic monetary policy on an open economy's inflation rate. These deficiencies are addressed in models to be outlined in chapters to follow.

5
Financial Flows, Interest Rates and Exchange Rates

This chapter introduces a new economy-wide framework for interpreting international interest differentials. It is based on borrowing and lending behaviour in small economies whose domestic capital markets have become more integrated with global capital markets. Using extended loanable funds analysis, the framework reconciles the main financial relations that link domestic and foreign interest rate – the Fisher effect, purchasing power parity and uncovered interest parity. It also shows that the reaction of foreign lenders to factors influencing an economy's creditworthiness is central to determining interest risk premia and how changing exchange rate expectations affect international interest differentials through borrowing and lending behaviour.

The chapter also examines the impact of domestic expenditure and output shocks on the exchange rate and external accounts in an intertemporal macroeconomic framework that incorporates international financial flows and forward looking behaviour. Exchange rate variation over time simply reflects the external price adjustment required to equalise foreign exchange flows arising from current and capital account transactions. By highlighting the role of foreign investors' expectations, the framework shows that whether increased domestic expenditure is on consumption or investment, whether output shocks are perceived as temporary or permanent, and whether residents' and foreigners' expectations are symmetric or asymmetric are central to the sustainability of exchange rates and external account balances.

5.1   Reconsidering interest rate parity

Pre-Keynesian loanable funds analysis suggested that interest rates in closed economies reflected the supply and demand for funds arising from domestic saving and investment behaviour. But with the international integration of financial markets over recent decades the scale of the international flow of funds has greatly increased with implications for cross border interest rate differentials. In financially liberalised open economies, investment spending can exceed domestic saving to the extent of foreign borrowing, or domestic saving exceed investment to the extent of foreign lending as demonstrated in the previous chapter.

The extant international finance literature is dominated by empirical studies that test the key theorems of interest rate behaviour, such as the Fisher interest rate effect, purchasing power parity and uncovered interest rate parity. These relationships are usually derived with reference to the arbitrage of returns on specific financial instruments, with equilibrium characterised in stock terms.[1] Typically, studies of interest parity, uncovered and real, test whether the same effective rate of return is earned on domestic and foreign securities with an equivalent term to maturity. In general, these studies are by nature partial and hence abstract from the international flow of funds and the saving-investment gap at the economy-wide level.

Saving and investment are recognised in the intertemporal approach of the previous chapter with its focus on the consumption and income effects of international borrowing and lending. Yet the intertemporal model neglects the effects of inflation, exchange rate expectations and risk on international interest differentials.

The following section introduces an alternative macroeconomic framework for interpreting the linkages between domestic saving and investment, international borrowing and lending, interest rates, inflation, risk, and exchange rate expectations for a small open economy. By reconciling the international flow of funds with the standard parity relationships of international finance, it thereby provides a means of identifying the factors that contribute to international interest differentials. The main international financial and macroeconomic relationships governing observed interest rates and the flow of funds through a small open economy are first developed as a basis for examining borrowing and lending behaviour under inflationary conditions. Next, different forms of time varying risk, including credit risk and country risk reveal how interest risk premia arise. The approach then shows how changing exchange rate expectations can further influence international borrowing and lending behaviour and hence cross-border interest differentials.

5.1.1 The Fisher effect and UIP

The accounting and behavioural relationships that link the nominal interest rate of a small open economy to the world interest rate via international financial flows, inflation rates and exchange rate expectations are

$$i_r = i_r^*$$ (5.1)

$$i^* = i_r^* + \pi^*$$ (5.2)

$$i = i_r + \pi$$ (5.3)

$$\overline{Y} - C(i) = S(i) = L(i); \qquad S_i > 0, L_i > 0$$ (5.4)

$$I = I(i, \beta) = B(i, \beta); \qquad I_i < 0, I_\beta > 0$$ (5.5)

$$B(i) - L(i) = CAB = B^*(i, i^*); \qquad B_i^* < 0, B_{i^*}^* < 0$$ (5.6)

$$\hat{E} = \frac{(e_{t+1} - e_t)}{e_t}$$ (5.7)

$$\pi - \pi^* = \Delta\pi = \hat{E}$$ (5.8)

$$B^*(i, i^*, \beta, \pi^*\Delta\pi) = L^*(i, i^*, \pi^*, \hat{E})$$ (5.9)

where i_r is the real domestic interest rate; $\overline{i}_r^*$ is the exogenous real world interest rate; i^* is the nominal world interest rate; i is the nominal domestic interest rate; π is expected domestic inflation; π^* is expected world inflation; $\overline{Y}$ is the small economy's given national income; C is its domestic consumption expenditure; S is domestic saving; L is domestic lending; I is real domestic investment; β is real domestic investment opportunities; *CAB* is the current account balance; *B* is the domestic demand for funds; B^* is the external borrowing requirement; $\hat{E}$ is expected currency depreciation; e_{t+1} and e_t are spot exchange rates at times $t+1$ and t; $\Delta \pi$ is domestic inflation in excess of world inflation; and L^* is foreign lending.

Consistent with the small-country variant of the intertemporal open economy model, domestic borrowers face a domestic real interest rate, i_r, set equal to the exogenous world interest rate, $\bar{i}_r^*$, in initial equilibrium as specified in equation (5.1). In addition, however, nominal domestic and world interest rates will reflect expectations of respective domestic and world inflation rates, according to the Fisher interest rate equations (5.2) and (5.3).

Standard loanable funds analysis suggests that domestic lending is positively related to the domestic interest rate and borrowing negatively related, as specified by equations (5.4) and (5.5). Saving, the residual between income and consumption, is lent by exchanging funds for interest earning financial instruments, such as bonds or certificates of deposit, which are issued by domestic borrowers to fund real investment spending. In a small open economy, facing a given world interest rate, an excess demand for funds by domestic residents creates an *ex ante* current account imbalance and an external borrowing requirement (equation (5.6)).

These relationships can now be graphically represented for a small open economy in loanable funds–interest rate space, as shown in Figure 5.1 which is consistent with the loanable funds analysis of the previous chapter. The left panel of Figure 5.1 shows the supply and demand for funds for a range of interest rates. The upward sloping schedule, L_0, in Figure 5.1 can be interpreted as a demand for interest earning assets schedule by domestic savers. The higher the domestic interest rate for a given level of wealth, the higher is the demand for interest earning assets, relative to the demand for other financial and real assets, such as equities and real estate. Domestic borrowers supply the interest earning financial investments on the other side of the market for loanable funds. They issue more instruments the lower the interest rate is, as conveyed by the downward sloping B_0 schedule. Total borrowing can exceed domestic lending at the world interest rate to the extent of foreign borrowing. The lower the world interest rate, the greater domestic residents' net demand for foreign funds, as shown by the downward sloping B_0^* schedule in the right side panel of Figure 5.1.

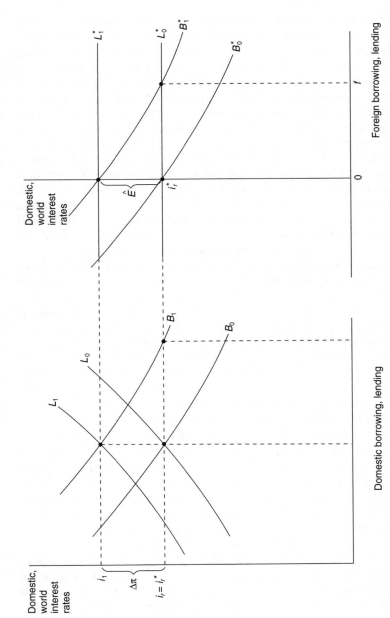

Figure 5.1 Interest parity and the international flow of funds

A rise in the economy's borrowing requirement, due for instance to increased real investment opportunities (a rise in β) shifts the B_0 schedule rightwards to B_1, giving rise to an *ex ante* external borrowing requirement of *Of* as shown in the right panel of Figure 5.1. If international capital mobility is perfect in the traditional sense, then foreign lenders fully meet the funding requirement by lending *Of* at i_0^*, the going world interest rate. Under these conditions, *ex ante* foreign lending behaviour is shown by the horizontal L_0^* schedule. Now consider the behaviour of interest rates and the international flow of funds after the onset of higher inflation in the small borrowing economy. The rise in domestic inflation exceeds the world inflation rate (assumed for the sake of exposition to be zero) by $\Delta \pi$. Domestic borrowing and lending are depicted in the first instance by the B_0 and L_0 schedules. Once higher domestic inflation begins however, saver-lenders would insist on being paid a higher nominal rate of return to compensate for the erosion in the value of their principal.

Meanwhile, the domestic demand for loanable funds rises from B_0 to B_1 (which for expositional purposes we assume is the same sized shift as for the above case of a rise in real investment opportunities). This increased demand for funds arises because borrowers also realise that it is possible to repay less capital in real terms during an inflation. As a result, the domestic nominal interest rate rises from i_0 to i_1 consistent with the Fisher interest rate effect, expressed in equation (5.3) above. It also causes the external borrowing schedule to shift up to B_1^*. The relationship between the domestic interest rate and inflation is accordingly depicted on the vertical axis of the left side panel of Figure 5.1.

Questions then arise about the behaviour of foreign lenders under these circumstances. This is where the relative purchasing power parity relation comes in (equation (5.8)). For, if domestic inflation is expected to exceed global inflation, then foreign lenders should also anticipate the exchange rate of the borrowing economy to depreciate, as predicted by the expected form of relative purchasing power parity.[2] Therefore, foreign lenders would require a higher rate of return on the domestic currency denominated bonds to compensate them for the capital losses incurred on maturity of those bonds.

Hence, the L_0^* schedule would shift up by the extent of the shift in the B_0^* schedule due to domestic inflation. In equilibrium, the demand for foreign funds equals the supply of foreign funds forthcoming, as expressed in equation (5.9) above. The result is that the domestic interest rate then differs from the foreign interest rate to the extent of both the expected inflation and the depreciation expected by foreign lenders, in accordance with the Fisher open, or uncovered interest rate relationship (UIP). That is,

$$i = \bar{i}_r^* + \Delta\pi = i^* + \hat{E} \tag{5.10}$$

5.1.2   Foreign borrowing, lending and risk

In the above analysis, foreign investors lend freely without being impeded by official restrictions such as exchange controls. Yet, even without exchange controls, risk-averse foreign investors may be unwilling to fully fund the borrowing requirements of domestic residents. Risk can now be introduced to the above analysis through the following equations:

$$F_t = \int_0^t B^*(t).dt \tag{5.11}$$

$$\rho = \rho(F_t, \mathcal{R}); \ \rho_{F_t} > 0, \ \rho_R > 0 \tag{5.12}$$

Equation (5.11) expresses the stock-flow relation between external borrowing and foreign debt levels, while equation (5.12) implies that foreign lenders perceive high current account deficits and rising foreign debt levels as signs of diminished creditworthiness, expecting an interest premium, ρ, to compensate for such risk. This risk rises with the level of foreign debt. Hence, the foreign lending schedule slopes upward, as shown by schedule L_0^* in Figure 5.2.

The more risk-averse foreign investors are to rising foreign debt, the steeper the slope of the L^* schedule and the higher the risk premium will be. Under these circumstances, international capital is imperfectly mobile. In addition, foreign lenders are unlikely to perceive debt instruments issued by the borrowing country as perfect substitutes for debt instruments issued in their home economies. For instance, even if such instruments were ostensibly the same in terms of their maturity structure, foreign lenders may be uncertain about political stability, the future tax treatment of their earnings or about capital controls being reimposed. Such factors are captured in the $\mathcal{R}$ term of equation (5.12).

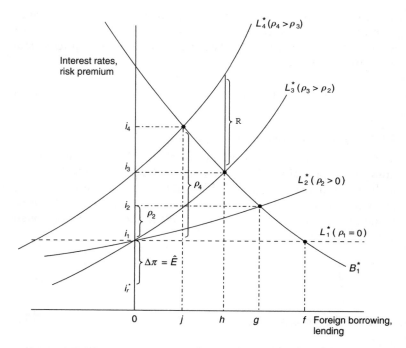

Figure 5.2   Foreign borrowing, lending, interest rates and creditworthiness

Figure 5.2 shows that for a given *ex ante* external borrowing requirement of *Of*, foreign funds to this amount will only be loaned in the limiting case of standard uncovered interest parity, that is, when $i_1 = i^* + \hat{E}$. However, to the extent that foreigners react negatively to rising foreign debt levels as reflected in the L_2^* schedule, then the amount actually lent will be *Og*. With this lesser amount of lending and capital inflow, the domestic interest rate of the borrowing country will be higher at i_2 which now differs from the foreign interest rate to the extent of expected depreciation and the debt related risk premium, ρ_2, as indicated on the vertical axis. That is, in general

$$i = i_r^* + \hat{E} + \rho \tag{5.13}$$

The more averse foreign lenders are to the rising external debt levels of borrower nations, the higher the equilibrium domestic interest rate, as shown by the foreign lending schedule L_3^* reflecting $\rho_3 > \rho_2$. For instance, the slope of the foreign lending schedule is likely to steepen following a downgrading in creditworthiness by international rating agencies. For instance, under these circumstances, *ex post* borrowing and lending would be *Oh* and the domestic interest rate i_3. Yet ρ also captures risk factors not directly related to the foreign indebtedness level such as overall country risk due for instance to political instability, through the shift variable $\mathcal{R}$. If the debtor economy experienced a political crisis for instance, foreign investors would suddenly become less willing to lend, causing the L_3^* schedule to rise to L_4^*. The cross-border interest differential would be higher at $(i_4 - i_r^*)$ and only *Oj* lending would have occurred *ex post*.

5.1.3 More on exchange rate expectations

Exchange rate expectations have so far played a role through the purchasing power parity relationship as it affects the lending decisions of foreigners when higher domestic inflation is expected. However, domestic borrowers and foreign lenders may also expect the exchange rate to depreciate for reasons other than a rise in domestic inflation over world inflation. These reasons could include the behaviour of the borrowing economy's terms of trade, the sustainability of its trade imbalance, or a change in the type of exchange rate regime adopted by the home economy.

It is now possible to incorporate the effects of changing exchange rate expectations for such reasons into this framework, as shown in Figure 5.3. Here, in the debt-averse case the domestic interest rate, i_1, initially exceeds the world rate, i_r^*, by the expected higher domestic inflation and the risk premium. However, foreign lenders now suddenly expect the exchange rate to depreciate by even more than the inflation differential, that is by $\Delta\hat{E}$, for the above mentioned reasons. As a result, they would insist on a higher rate of return on domestic currency denominated bonds to compensate them for the capital losses on maturity of those bonds. Hence the L_2^* schedule shifts up to L_3^* by the full extent of the further expected depreciation, $\Delta\hat{E}$.

At the same time, domestic borrowers with the same expectations of currency depreciation realize that a future weakening of the home economy's exchange rate confers a capital gain on the foreign

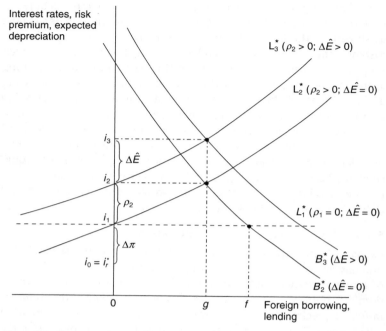

Figure 5.3   Interest rates, risk and expected depreciation

exchange acquired from foreign lenders in exchange for bonds
denominated in domestic currency. This would effectively lower the
cost to residents of external borrowing and hence increase the issue of
home currency denominated bonds. In Figure 5.3, this is depicted as an
outward shift of B_2^* to B_3^*. In sum, therefore, the difference between the
observed domestic interest rate and the foreign interest rate can be
decomposed into its main components, the inflation gap, risk and
further expected exchange rate depreciation, consistent with the
interest parity relationship when stated with a time-varying risk
premium. That is

$$i = i_r^* + \Delta\pi + \rho + \Delta\hat{E} \tag{5.14}$$

5.2 Exchange rate behaviour in an intertemporal framework

A primary function of the balance of payments accounts is to provide a statistical record in flow terms of the supply and demand for an economy's currency. It is the nominal exchange rate itself which ensures the equality in principle between the current and capital balances in these accounts. An economy with a current account deficit (surplus) has an excess demand (supply) for foreign currency which is satisfied by an excess supply (demand) of foreign currency, provided through the matching capital account surplus (deficit). Hence, it follows that both current and capital account flows should simultaneously be taken into account when modelling exchange rate behaviour. Yet this has not been explicitly recognised in asset market models because of their focus on stock adjustment and financial markets.

In contrast, this section develops an alternative flow model of the exchange rate and the external accounts. It combines financial and real influences on the exchange rate by linking foreign exchange flows that are related to intertemporal current and capital account transactions to economy wide production and expenditure behaviour. It first develops the basic framework to be used subsequently to analyse the impact of private domestic investment and output shocks on the exchange rate and external accounts when the expectations of foreigners and residents are symmetric and asymmetric. The model is then compared to the Fisherian intertemporal framework of the previous chapter which abstracts from exchange rate adjustment and the expectations of foreign investors.

5.2.1 The analytical framework

On the real side, the macroeconomic accounting relations underpinning the subsequent analytical framework to be developed are

$$A = C + I \tag{5.15}$$

$$A - Y = CAD \tag{5.16}$$

where A is absorption or national expenditure, C is consumption, I is investment, Y is national output or income, CAD is the current account deficit.

Exchange rate, spending and income relations

The real exchange rate, ϕ, influences aggregate output and expenditure and hence the current account balance. It is defined as

$$\phi = \frac{eP^*}{P} \tag{5.17}$$

where e is the nominal effective exchange rate, P^* is the foreign price level and P is the domestic price level. In what follows, it is assumed that the foreign and domestic price levels are stable. Hence, as is usual in other macroeconomic models, movements in the nominal exchange rate are solely responsible for real exchange rate variation over shorter periods. The national expenditure function can then be written as

$$A = A(\phi(e); C(i, Y), I(i)) \quad A_e < 0, A_i < 0, A_y > 0 \tag{5.18}$$

Domestic consumption and investment spending are influenced by interest rates and income in the normal way. However, the total expenditure of resident households and firms in an open economy includes spending on imported goods and services whose prices are initially set in foreign currency. A stronger exchange rate lowers the domestic currency price of imports, increasing import demand and total expenditure. Hence, a downward sloping expenditure schedule can be drawn in exchange rate-national expenditure space as shown in Figure 5.4.

The aggregate supply function is specified as

$$Y = Y(\phi(e); \ell(w), K, \tau) \quad Y_e > 0, Y_w < 0, Y_k > 0, Y_\tau > 0 \tag{5.19}$$

where L, K and τ ; are the factor inputs labour, capital and technology used to produce national output. Hours worked, l, depend on the prevailing real wage, w, presumed invariant over the short run. Nominal exchange rate depreciations improve competitiveness (ϕ) and hence encourage higher exports of goods and services. Since national product includes that part of output sold abroad as exports, total output is positively related to the nominal exchange rate and can therefore be represented by an upward sloping schedule in exchange rate–output space, as also shown in Figure 5.4. In the absence of capital flows, the trade (current) account is balanced and the nominal

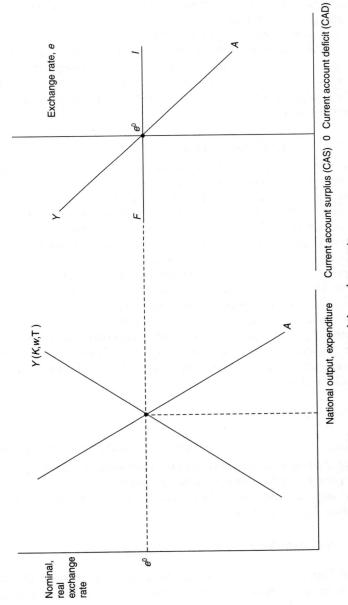

Figure 5.4 Output, expenditure, the current account and the exchange rate

exchange rate is at equilibrium at the point where national expenditure equals national output.

The negatively sloped *YA* schedule in the right panel of Figure 5.4 shows the excess demand for foreign currency arising from divergences between domestic expenditure and income. The stronger the exchange rate, the higher the excess demand for goods and services, and hence the greater the economy's net demand for foreign currency for current account purposes.

5.2.2   Intertemporal relations

To complete the model, it is necessary to add some basic intertemporal relations. Consistent with standard Fisherian intertemporal analysis, the time frame is limited to two periods only, the present and the future. As it is assumed that international capital is perfectly mobile, there are no risk premia or barriers to foreign investment in bonds. Foreign exchange simply flows into the small economy whenever foreign investors expect the total return from holding newly-issued host-economy bonds to exceed the world interest rate.

In this floating exchange rate model, the central bank does not intervene in the foreign exchange market. Monetary policy is conducted by pegging the domestic interest rate, i, to the world interest rate, i^*, at all times. The differential between effective returns on domestic versus foreign bonds in period 1 is then only attributable to expected exchange rate movements, according to the open interest parity relationship,

$$i^1 + \hat{a} = i^{*1} \tag{5.20}$$

where $\hat{a} = \dfrac{-(e_E^2 - e^1)}{e^1}$ with $\hat{a}$ being the exchange rate appreciation expected over the duration from the beginning of period 1 to the end of period 2, e_E^2 the expected exchange rate at the end of period 2 and e^1 the spot exchange rate at the beginning of period 1. Hence, the capital inflow function can be written as

$$KAS^1 = KAS(\hat{a}; i^{1,2} = i^{*1,2}) \qquad KAS_{\hat{a}} > 0 \tag{5.21}$$

The supply of foreign exchange made available through the capital account to finance any current account deficit attributable to an excess of domestic expenditure over domestic production in the first of two periods depends on the take up by foreigners of domestic debt instruments that are issued in the local currency to fund increased expenditure. This increase in foreign debt, dF^*, plus interest obligations to foreigners must be repaid in the second period. Hence to satisfy the intertemporal budget constraint

$$CAD^1 + \frac{CAD^2}{(1+i^*)} = KAS^1 + \frac{KAS^2}{(1+i^*)} = dF^{*1} + \frac{dF^{*2}}{(1+i^*)} = 0 \qquad (5.22)$$

Capital inflow to finance output-expenditure gaps is depicted in Figure 5.4 by the schedule labelled *FI*.

5.2.3 Expenditure shocks

Having established these foundations, it is possible to show how strictly macroeconomic factors can simultaneously influence current account deficits, capital flows and the exchange rate. First, suppose there is additional domestic investment expenditure by resident firms because the real prospective return on newly installed capital is expected to exceed the world interest rate. This shifts the left panel expenditure schedule in Figure 5.5 rightwards in period 1 from A^0 to A^1.

If foreigners had these expectations, yet the nominal exchange rate actually tended to rise above e^0 as domestic investment expenditure increased, an international interest differential would open up to the extent that an exchange rate appreciation was expected in the second period, in line with the predicted expansion of output and reversal of the initial CAD. This momentary differential would remain open until all the foreign currency required to fund the output-expenditure imbalance was forthcoming and the equilibrium exchange rate of e^0 was restored. This follows because the segment of the Y^1A^1 schedule labelled fe^1 is actually the supply of foreign currency curve read from right to left, provided the exchange rate at the end of period 2 is expected to be the same as at the beginning of period 1.

The above model also suggests that real exchange rate movements may be related to changes in overall domestic saving behaviour. Decreased thrift resulting from higher domestic consumption, for instance, is likely to depreciate the nominal, and hence real, exchange rate over the medium term, to the extent that foreigners are unlikely to persistently underwrite such behaviour.

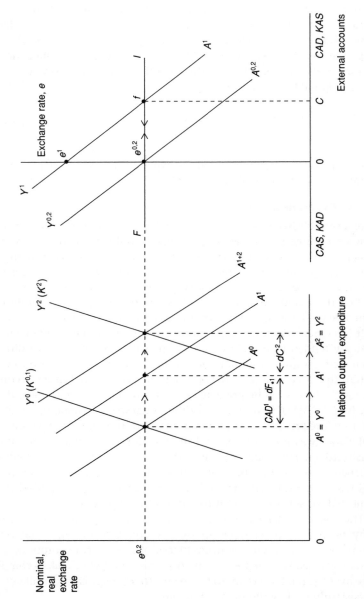

Figure 5.5 Increased private investment and external adjustment

In general, if foreign investors expect additional domestic expenditure in one period to generate the minimum necessary extra production for repayment in the next, then in this framework they expect the *YA* schedule to return to its initial position and the exchange rate to be at the same level then as at the outset. An initial *ex ante* CAD is therefore sustainable in the sense that foreigners fully finance it and the exchange rate does not immediately depreciate to eliminate it.

5.2.4 Asymmetric expectations

Thus far, it has been assumed that resident and foreign investors have symmetric expectations about the prospective values of output, expenditure and the exchange rate. But, it may be the case that forward looking foreign investors are less optimistic than residents about the productivity of extra domestic investment spending. Hence, foreigners may not provide the full amount of foreign exchange needed to finance an *ex ante* expenditure–output gap if their views of the future differ from those of residents. Under these conditions, the *ex ante* current account deficit measured as the gap between output and desired expenditure is not fully sustainable.

With reference to Figure 5.6, if foreigners deem, contrary to resident investors, that part of an initial excess domestic demand is unproductive, then only part of the associated demand for foreign currency is satisfied, such that the nominal exchange rate immediately depreciates to e^{2*}. In the figure, the CAD which manifests with asymmetric expectations about the productivity of additional domestic investment is shown by distance OC'. Again, what becomes apparent is that current account deficits only persist as long as foreign investors allow them to. By raising the real exchange rate, exchange rate depreciation thereby reduces domestic expenditure and stimulates additional production. In the longer run, of course, exchange rate changes will affect the domestic price level and hence real wages and aggregate output. However, as the focus is on the short run, such effects are ignored here.

Alternatively, it is possible that foreigners' expectations about the adjustment process may be too optimistic. For instance, had foreigners mistakenly financed the full ex ante increase in the CAD of OC on the presumption that the *YA* schedule would at least return to its original

102

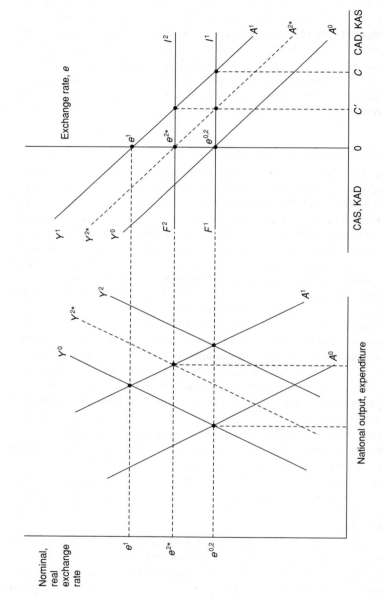

Figure 5.6 Asymmetric expectations, current account sustainability and the exchange rate

position and not that shown by the $Y^{2*}A^{2*}$ schedule, then they would suffer losses on bond holdings due to eventual currency depreciation. This follows from the assumption that the domestic debt instruments are issued in the local currency.

5.2.5 Output shocks

This framework can also be used to show the external effects of supply-side shocks. With reference to Figure 5.7, if there is a temporary real disturbance which adversely affects domestic production, the output schedule shifts leftward. For given domestic spending, including the maintenance by residents of consumption spending in line with permanent income, the output-expenditure gap would tend to widen. If foreign investors also viewed the output slump as temporary, they too would expect production to return to its former volume. The future YA schedule, and hence nominal exchange rate, would therefore be expected to coincide with the initial YA schedule and exchange rate. Foreigners would therefore willingly fund the full *ex ante* output–expenditure imbalance allowing the CAD to rise to OC. Such behaviour is consistent with the notion that current account deficits may allow for smoothing of consumption in the face of temporary income fluctuations.[3] Again, however, with asymmetric expectations foreigners may initially misjudge a supply-side shock and expect output to only revert to, say, Y^{2*} in the future as shown by the dashed line in the left panel of the figure. Under these circumstances, the exchange rate would immediately depreciate from e^0 to e^{2*} and the CAD only reach OC' in the first period. In the above example, current account deficits only emerge following supply-side shocks if both residents and foreigners recognise the shocks as temporary. On the contrary, if a disturbance is considered permanent by residents and foreigners alike, the exchange rate would eventually have to depreciate to e^1.

In general, the supply of foreign exchange made available in the first instance to finance any excess domestic expenditure over the domestic production depends on foreigners' expectations about the dynamic paths of production and spending and hence on the current account balance and its implications for the future exchange rate. Contrary to the emphasis in the literature on asset market relations and the capital account, this implies the current account is central to the long run determination of the exchange rate.

104

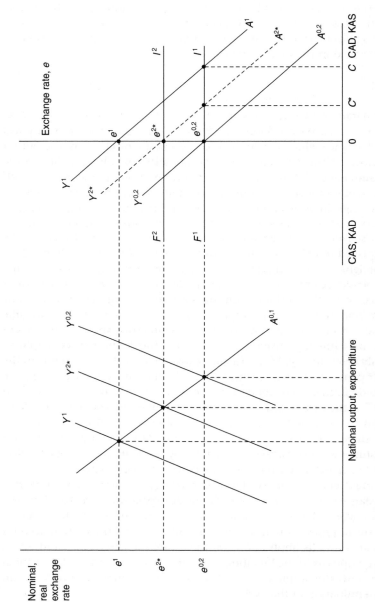

Figure 5.7   An output shock, consumption smoothing and external adjustment

5.3 Conclusion

This chapter has further explored the linkages between international financial flows, interest rates, exchange rates and other macroeconomic variables. As discussed in the previous chapter, empirical tests of the partial theorems of international finance encompassed by the analysis in section 5.2 frequently fail to provide support for a variety of reasons. For instance, purchasing power parity will not hold one-for-one if the underlying cross-border arbitrage in goods markets on which it is premised is incomplete, or if the national price indices used to measure respective inflation rates are dissimilar in their coverage. The Fisher effect and uncovered interest parity relations will also be weakened by complications arising from transactions costs, tax treatment and incomplete arbitrage in asset markets. In addition, these relations implicitly assume that expectations are formed rationally by all domestic and foreign borrowers and lenders and that there are no information asymmetries.

This chapter has provided another way of understanding how observed international interest differentials arise by outlining a macroeconomic framework for interpreting interest rate parity and deviations from it. With international borrowing and lending activity as its central focus, it modelled the macroeconomic linkages between inflation expectations, risk, exchange rate expectations and international interest rate differentials. By reconciling traditional loanable funds analysis with other key relationships that govern interest rate behaviour, it has been shown that the differential between a small borrower economy's domestic interest rate and the world interest rate can be decomposed into the gap between domestic and world inflation, a risk premium and further exchange rate depreciation expected by residents and foreigners alike.

The reaction of foreign lenders was shown to be central to determining the size of the interest risk premium paid by borrowers in a small open economy. This risk premium could vary over time for a variety of reasons related to the economy's creditworthiness or non-economic factors, such as political instability. At the same time, through their impact on both excess domestic borrowing and foreign lending behaviour, changing exchange rate expectations may also significantly influence interest rate differentials.

Even though there are many contending exchange rate models in the literature, little consensus about the main causes of exchange rate fluctuations has yet emerged. Indeed, many economists and practitioners continue to subscribe to the view that foreign exchange markets are inherently unstable and prone to irrational influences. Alternatively, this chapter also proposed a simple flow model of exchange determination premised on macroeconomic fundamentals and well-informed market participants, which is not inconsistent with the efficiency notions of modern finance theory.

As an intertemporal model, it differs in a number of ways from the two-period Fisherian approach to the open economy. The most fundamental point of difference is that it makes the exchange rate central to intertemporal balance of payments analysis, whereas the Fisherian approach neglects the exchange rate altogether, instead emphasising the roles of saving, investment and the current account. The standard intertemporal approach also implicitly assumes that foreigners automatically and indiscriminately fund all domestic *ex ante* saving–investment imbalances even though, realistically, foreign investors must continually make judgements about whether the additional expenditure they finance in debtor countries has the potential to generate sufficient production to allow for eventual repayment of their funds.

Finally, this model provides another dimension to the notion of current account sustainability, usually employed to characterise the time path of the current account deficit. External account imbalances expressed in foreign exchange terms over any given period reflect how much of residents' desired excess expenditure is satisfied by foreign investors making judgements about the future domestic income such expenditure will sustain. In other words, current account deficits only arise when foreign investors sanction them on the understanding that such deficits will eventually be self-financing. Accordingly, unsustainable *ex ante* deficits arising from strictly domestic factors would be checked by movements in nominal exchange rate movements. If not, then foreign investors bear the risk of any exchange rate adjustment which follows.

6
Macroeconomic Policy in the Open Economy

In the theory presented so far, minimal attention has been given to the impact of macroeconomic policy in open economies. The best-known macroeconomic model for examining the operation of fiscal and monetary policy in an open economy is that proposed by Fleming (1962) and Mundell (1963). The Mundell–Fleming (MF) model is an open economy extension of the textbook Keynesian framework and links international financial capital flows, interest differentials, exchange rates, competitiveness, exports, imports and national income. The popularity of MF analysis stems from its conclusions about the effectiveness of monetary and fiscal policy in stabilising national income under alternative exchange rate regimes.

In the exposition to follow, discussion centres mainly on the floating exchange rate version of the MF model with internationally mobile financial flows as these conditions are most relevant in current circumstances.[1] The main predictions of the approach are first derived mathematically and then presented diagrammatically with particular reference to the significance of international financial flows and the external accounts. The chapter concludes with a critical evaluation of the model.

6.1 The Mundell–Fleming model

In its basic version, the MF model assumes a small open economy with a perfectly elastic aggregate supply curve, static exchange rate expectations and perfect capital mobility. On the real side of the economy, the model assumes unemployed resources and a fixed price level. On the financial side there are only three financial assets (rows (2), (4) and (7) of Figure 2.4) – domestic base money which is non-substitutable for foreign base money, domestic and foreign bonds which are perfectly substitutable for each other, and foreign reserves (used to manage the exchange rate in the fixed exchange rate version of the model).

Since static exchange rate expectations mean that the exchange rate is not expected to deviate from its present level, the assumption of perfect capital mobility implies that home and foreign interest rates (r and r^* respectively) will always be equal, both in nominal and real terms. Consistent with its Keynesian underpinnings, gross domestic product is demand-determined and there is no inflation. Part of total absorption is autonomous, while the rest depends negatively on the domestic interest rate, through domestic private investment, and positively on national income, through the propensity of households to consume. Government expenditure may be either public consumption or public investment and is included within the autonomous component of total spending along with private autonomous consumption and investment.

Net exports (or the current account in the absence of net income or transfers paid abroad) are a function of the domestic propensity to import and the exchange rate. Given the fixed price level assumption, nominal exchange rate changes translate one for one to real exchange rate changes since the real exchange rate again defined as eP^*/P. The Marshall–Lerner condition is assumed to hold.

Equilibrium in the money market is given by the stock equality of real money demand (L), which depends negatively on the domestic interest rate and positively on real income, and the real money supply, (M^s).

6.2   Expenditure and monetary shocks

This section now mathematically examines the comparative statics of the MF model under floating exchange rates with varying degrees of capital mobility.[2] Goods market equilibrium may be written as the condition that total injections equal leakages.

$$\overline{A} + I(r) + X(e) = S(Y) + M(Y, e) \tag{6.1}$$

where $I_r < 0, X_e > 0, 0 < S_y < 1, 0 < M_y < 1, M_e < 0$. $\overline{A}$ denotes total autonomous expenditure including private and public consumption and private and public investment expenditure; the other variables are as defined above and in Chapter 2.

Money market equilibrium is given by the stock equality of real money demand and the real money supply:

$$M^s = L(Y, r) \tag{6.2}$$

$$L_y > 0, L_r < 0$$

The external accounts under a floating exchange rate can also be expressed as

$$B = X(e) - M(Y, e) + KAB(r) = 0 \tag{6.3}$$

Total differentiation of equations (6.1), (6.2) and (6.3) yields, after some rearrangement, the following matrix:

$$\begin{bmatrix} S_y + M_y & -I_r & (M_e - X_e) \\ L_y & L_r & 0 \\ M_y & -KAB_r & (M_e - X_e) \end{bmatrix} \begin{bmatrix} dy \\ dr \\ de \end{bmatrix} = \begin{bmatrix} d\overline{A} \\ dM^s \\ 0 \end{bmatrix}$$

The coefficient matrix may be inverted to yield

$$\begin{bmatrix} dY \\ dr \\ de \end{bmatrix} = \begin{bmatrix} \dfrac{L_r(M_e - X_e)}{D} & \dfrac{(I_r - KAB_r)(M_e - X_e)}{D} & \dfrac{-L_r(M_e - X_e)}{D} \\ \dfrac{-L_y(M_e - X_e)}{D} & \dfrac{S_y(M_e - X_e)}{D} & \dfrac{L_y(M_e - X_e)}{D} \\ \dfrac{-(L_y KAB_r + L_r M_y)}{D} & \dfrac{KAB_r(S_y + M_y) - I_r M_y}{D} & \dfrac{-L_r(S_y + M_y) + L_y I_r}{D} \end{bmatrix} \begin{bmatrix} d\overline{A} \\ dM^s \\ 0 \end{bmatrix}$$

where the determinant of the coefficient matrix

$$D = (M_e - X_e)(L_r S_y - L_y KAB_r + I_r L_y) > 0$$

6.2.1 Increased autonomous expenditure

It follows that the multipliers for a change in autonomous expenditure are

$$\frac{dY}{d\overline{A}} = \frac{L_r}{L_rS_y - L_yKAB_r + I_rL_y} > 0$$

$$\frac{dr}{d\overline{A}} = \frac{-L_y}{L_rS_y - L_yKAB_r + I_rL_y} > 0$$

$$\frac{de}{d\overline{A}} = \frac{-(L_yKAB_r + L_rM_y)}{(M_e - X_e)(L_rS_y - L_yKAB_r + I_rL_y)} \begin{matrix} > \\ < \end{matrix} 0$$

The last is ambiguous since L_yKAB is positive and L_rM_y is negative.

The above results suggest that an increase in autonomous expenditure, including increased public spending due to discretionary fiscal expansion raises both the equilibrium level of income and interest rate. The effect on the exchange rate is ambiguous. If financial capital flows are perfectly mobile in the MF sense, $KAB_r \to \infty$. Hence, the above multipliers under floating exchange rates reduce to

$$\frac{dY}{d\overline{A}} = 0$$

$$\frac{dr}{d\overline{A}} = 0$$

$$\frac{de}{d\overline{A}} = \frac{1}{M_e - X_e} < 0$$

Therefore under floating exchange rates, increased autonomous expenditure is ineffective in raising national income but appreciates the exchange rate.

Alternatively, if financial capital is completely immobile, $KAB_r = 0$, and the multipliers reduce to

$$\frac{dY}{d\overline{A}} = \frac{L_r}{L_rS_y + I_rL_y} > 0$$

$$\frac{dr}{d\overline{A}} = \frac{-L_y}{L_rS_y + I_rL_y} > 0$$

$$\frac{de}{d\overline{A}} = \frac{-L_rM_y}{(M_e - X_e)(L_rS_y + I_rL_y)} > 0$$

Modifying the perfect capital mobility assumption therefore allows autonomous expenditure increases to impact positively on income and the domestic interest rate.

6.2.2 Monetary expansion

From the matrix, the multipliers from a monetary expansion reduce to

$$\frac{dY}{dM^s} = \frac{I_r - KAB_r}{L_r S_y - L_y KAB_r + I_r L_y} > 0$$

$$\frac{dr}{dM^s} = \frac{S_y}{L_r S_y - L_y KAB_r + I_r L_y} < 0$$

$$\frac{de}{dM^s} = \frac{KAB_r(S_y + M_y) - I_r M_y}{(M_e - X_e)(L_r S_y - L_y KAB_r + I_r L_y)} > 0$$

Hence expansionary monetary policy raises equilibrium income, lowers the domestic interest rate and depreciates the exchange rate.

With perfect capital mobility, $KAB_r \to \infty$, the multipliers are

$$\frac{dY}{dM^s} = \frac{1}{L_y} > 0$$

$$\frac{dr}{dM^s} = 0$$

$$\frac{de}{dM^s} = \frac{S_y + M_y}{-(M_e - X_e)L_y} > 0$$

This suggests that monetary policy is effective in raising income and depreciating the exchange rate, but that perfect capital mobility ensures the domestic interest rate does not change.

Again, varying the capital mobility assumptions, if $KAB_r = 0$, the multipliers reduce to

$$\frac{dY}{dM^s} = \frac{I_r}{L_r S_y + I_r L_y} > 0$$

$$\frac{dr}{dM^s} = \frac{S_y}{L_r S_y + I_r L_y} < 0$$

$$\frac{de}{dM^s} = \frac{-I_r M_y}{(M_e - X_e)(L_r S_y + I_r L_y)} > 0$$

Under these conditions, monetary expansion raises equilibrium income, lowers the domestic interest rate and depreciates the exchange rate.

6.2.3   Stability analysis

Stability analysis concerns the time paths of variables when the economy is out of equilibrium. To conduct stability analysis it is therefore necessary to make assumptions about how the key variables in the MF model behave when away from their equilibrium values. Accordingly, the above version of the MF model may be expressed in dynamic terms as

$$\frac{dY}{dt} = \alpha_1[\overline{A} + I(r) + X(e) - S(Y) - M(Y, e)] \tag{6.4}$$

$$\frac{dr}{dt} = \alpha_2[L(Y, r) - M^s] \tag{6.5}$$

$$\frac{de}{dt} = -\alpha_3[X(e) - M(Y, e) + KAB(r)] \tag{6.6}$$

Equation (6.4) suggests that income adjustment is proportional to the gap between injections (autonomous expenditure, interest sensitive investment and exports) and leakages (saving and imports). The speed of adjustment is determined by reaction coefficient α_1. Equation (6.5) implies that if real money demand rises above the real money supply then the interest rate rises at a rate determined by reaction co-efficient α_2. Equation (6.6) states that the exchange rate appreciates at a speed governed by reaction coefficient α_3 as capital inflow exceeds net exports.

The above implicit functions can be replaced with linear approximations in the neighbourhood of equilibrium, such that the equations may be rewritten in linear homogeneous form as

$$\frac{dY}{dt} = \alpha_1[-(S_y + M_y)(Y - \overline{Y}) + I_r(r - \overline{r}) + (M_e - X_e)(e - \overline{e})]$$
$$\frac{dr}{dt} = \alpha_2[L_y(Y - \overline{Y}) + L_r(r - \overline{r})]$$
$$\frac{de}{dt} = \alpha_3[-M_y(Y - \overline{Y}) + KAB_r(r - \overline{r}) - (M_e - X_e)(e - \overline{e})]$$

where $\overline{Y}, \overline{r}, \overline{e}$ denote final equilibrium values.

Solutions to these differential equations must express the values of the variables as functions of time and be of the form

$$Y = \overline{Y} + \beta_1 E^{qt} \tag{6.7}$$

$$r = \overline{r} + \beta_2 E^{qt} \tag{6.8}$$

$$e = \overline{e} + \beta_3 E^{qt} \tag{6.9}$$

where E is the exponential. If Y, r and e approach their equilibrium values $\overline{Y}, \overline{r}, \overline{e}$, the system is stable and for this to occur the term q (the characteristic root) must be negative for the dynamic component of the right hand expression to approach zero through time. Differentiating equations (6.7), (6.8) and (6.9) with respect to time yields

$$\frac{dY}{dt} = q\beta_1 E^{qt} = q(Y - \overline{Y})$$

$$\frac{dr}{dt} = q\beta_2 E^{qt} = q(r - \overline{r})$$

$$\frac{de}{dt} = q\beta_3 E^{qt} = q(e - \overline{e})$$

Substituting $q(Y - \overline{Y})$, $q(i - \overline{i})$ and $q(e - \overline{e})$ for $\frac{dY}{dr}, \frac{dr}{dt}$ and $\frac{de}{dt}$ respectively yields the matrix equation.

$$\begin{bmatrix} q + \alpha_1(S_y + M_y) & -\alpha_1 I_r & \alpha_1(M_e - X_e) \\ -\alpha_2 L_y & q - \alpha_2 L_r & 0 \\ -\alpha_3 M_y & \alpha_3 KAB_r & q - \alpha_3(M_e - X_e) \end{bmatrix} \begin{bmatrix} Y - \overline{Y} \\ r - \overline{r} \\ e - \overline{e} \end{bmatrix} = 0$$

The characteristic matrix cannot have an inverse, otherwise displacements from equilibrium would be zero. The characteristic equation derived from the characteristic determinant is

$$q^2 + [\alpha_1(S_y + M_y) - \alpha_2 L_r + \alpha_3(M_e - X_e)]q^2 + [-\alpha_1\alpha_2 L_r(S_y + M_y) -$$

$$\alpha_1\alpha_3(S_y + M_y)(M_e - X_e) + \alpha_2\alpha_3 L_r(M_e - X_e)] + \alpha_1\alpha_2\alpha_3(M_e - X_e)$$

$$(L_r S_y - L_y KAB_r + I_r L_y) = 0$$

All coefficients must be positive for stability to prevail. Since S_y, M_y and I_r are positive and L_r and I_r are negative, this condition is met provided that exchange depreciation reduces net imports (i.e. $M_e - X_e < 0$) in accordance with the Marshall–Lerner condition.

6.3   Graphical analysis

The standard effectiveness results set out above are usually derived graphically using the familiar *IS–LM–BP* framework. Shown below is the conventional presentation, augmented by a supplementary framework, based on the same Keynesian assumptions, which allows us to trace more explicitly the effects of autonomous expenditure and monetary shocks on the trade account, as well as the saving–investment imbalance.

Consider first the implications of an autonomous spending increase on the trade account under the assumptions of a floating exchange rate and perfect capital mobility. In terms of *IS–LM–BP* analysis, the *IS* curve moves to the right putting upward pressure on the domestic interest rate. However, this incipient interest rate rise attracts foreign capital, appreciating the currency. Hence, the exchange rate is assumed to be entirely capital account driven. The loss of competitiveness thereby crowds out net exports shifting back the *IS* curve to its initial position.

Accompanying the *IS–LM–BP* diagram is what we will term an *NS– NX* framework. This supplementary framework highlights the effects of various shocks on the economy's saving-investment and external account imbalances which, as demonstrated in Chapter 2, must be equal to each other *ex post*. In full equilibrium the saving-investment and external account imbalances must of course also be equal *ex ante*. The upward sloping *NS* schedule shows net saving and is drawn for a given autonomous expenditure and domestic interest rate. An increase in income raises net saving as the marginal propensity to consume is less than unity and investment is autonomous.

Hence the slope of this schedule is determined by the marginal propensity to save which lies between zero and unity. The downward sloping *NX* schedule is drawn for a given level of autonomous exports and competitiveness. This schedule shows that as income rises, imports increase and hence the trade deficit widens. Its slope is minus the marginal propensity to import. An improvement in competitiveness shifts the net export schedule to the right as the Marshall–Lerner condition is satisfied. For ease of exposition of the comparative static effects on the trade account and saving–investment imbalance, it is assumed that in initial equilibrium the trade account is balanced.

Therefore, an increase in autonomous expenditure as shown in Figure 6.1 shifts the *IS* curve to the right and also shifts the net saving

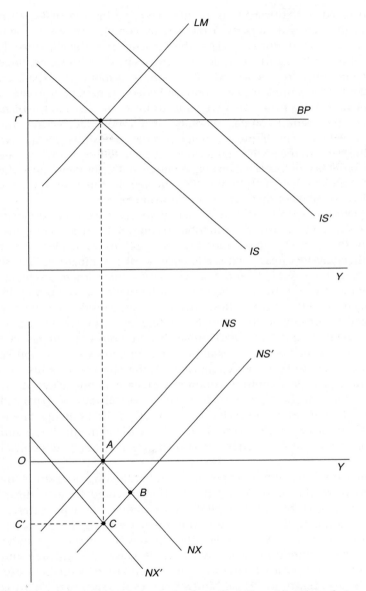

Figure 6.1   Domestic expenditure shocks in the MF model with perfect capital mobility

(*NS*) schedule rightward from point *A* to *B*, raising the trade deficit through increased imports. However, as competitiveness worsens because capital inflow appreciates the exchange rate, the *NX* schedule shifts left such that the trade deficit increases by *OCN*. However, there is no net effect on income. On the contrary, a monetary expansion under these assumptions has a powerful effect on national income. A rightward shift of the *LM* curve tends to lower interest rates, which, given the perfect capital mobility assumption, depreciates the exchange rate. This improves competitiveness and shifts the *IS* curve to the right. In the *NS–NX* framework, the incipient lower interest rate has no effect on autonomous expenditure but only depreciates the exchange rate which shifts the *NX* schedule. In this case, the trade deficit unambiguously improves as shown in Figure 6.2.

Domestic expenditure and monetary shocks have quite different effects if capital is assumed immobile (Figures 6.3 and 6.4) compared with the perfect capital mobility assumption, as earlier shown mathematically. Again with reference to the standard *IS–LM–BP* diagram, the effects of various shocks on the interest rate, exchange rate, income and the trade account can be modelled by varying the slope of the *BP* curve. For illustrative purposes, consider the effect of capital immobility ($KAB_r = 0$) in the limiting case of a vertical *BP* curve, showing that capital flows are completely unresponsive to interest rate changes, as may occur for example for economies with prohibitive exchange controls. In such circumstances, the external accounts only comprise a trade account in common with earlier approaches. If the exchange rate floats, the trade balance will always be balanced through changes in the exchange rate itself. If the exchange rate is fixed, the trade deficit becomes the balance of payments deficit and would usually be financed by a rundown in the central bank's official reserves.

Increased autonomous expenditure under floating rates shifts the *IS* curve to the right raising the trade deficit and *NS* also shifts. However, with immobile capital the exchange rate depreciates to restore a balanced trade account, thus further shifting the *IS* curve as well as the *BP* and *NX* curves. Finally, a money supply increase under the same assumptions worsens the trade balance as income and imports rise. This depreciates the currency and thereby further shifts the *IS* curve rightward. The *BP* and *NX* curves also shift to the right as shown.

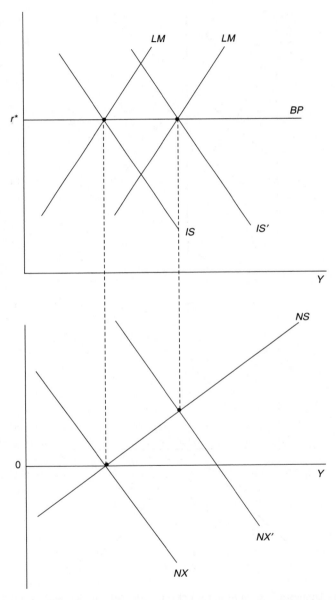

Figure 6.2   Monetary expansion in the MF model with perfect capital mobility

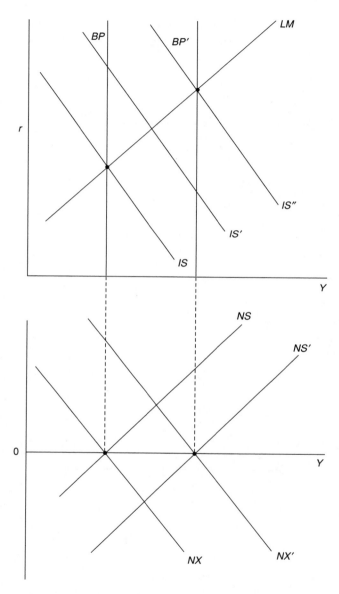

Figure 6.3 Domestic expenditure shocks in the MF model with capital immobility

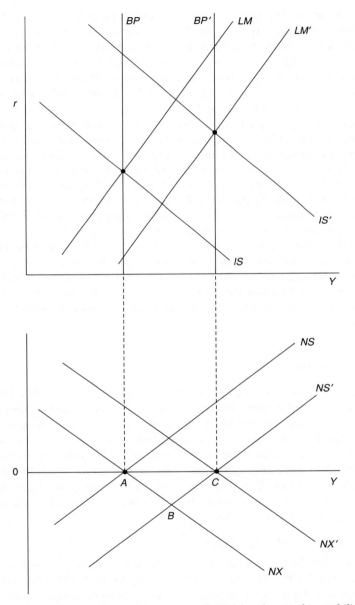

Figure 6.4 Monetary expansion in the MF model with capital immobility

The basic MF model may also be used to provide a theoretical rationale for linking expansionary fiscal policy, as manifested in wider budget deficits, to trade or current account deficits. This causal link, termed the 'twin deficits' hypothesis, is a specific case of the more general case which treats the comparative static effects of increased domestic expenditure under floating exchange rates with capital mobility as outlined in Figure 6.2.

Budget deficits may widen as either public consumption or public investment expenditure increases or because income taxes are cut. Public expenditure increases directly augment autonomous expenditure whereas tax cuts are assumed to stimulate household consumption expenditure. Either way, consistent with the MF approach, bigger budget deficits initially put upward pressure on the domestic interest rate which induces capital inflow. This then appreciates the nominal exchange rate, crowds out net exports and widens the *CAD*.

Although the augmented *IS–LM–BP* framework has been used to examine the comparative statics of expenditure and monetary shocks under a floating exchange rate with polar degrees of capital mobility, it is also possible to adapt the approach for a fixed rate environment. A summary of the main results under both regimes is included in Table 6.1.

6.4   Limitations

There are a number of problems with the MF specifications of both the real and financial sides of the economy. Taken together these shortcomings and inconsistencies limit its usefulness as a vehicle for understanding the nature and significance of external account determination, notwithstanding its popularity as the ruling textbook framework for interpreting international macroeconomic policy issues. These limitations can be traced to flaws in the underlying assumptions of the basic model, many of which have only been addressed piecemeal in the open economy literature.

6.4.1   Goods market specification

Starting with the real side, the heart of traditional Keynesian analysis, the standard MF model implicitly assumes all goods are internationally tradable and the economy is small. However, domestic producers and consumers are not price takers in the dependent economy sense, which

Table 6.1 Expenditure and money supply increases under floating and fixed exchange rate regimes

	Floating exchange rate $KAB_r \to \infty$	Floating exchange rate $KAB_r = 0$	Fixed exchange rate $KAB_r \to \infty$	Fixed exchange rate $KAB_r = 0$
Expenditure increase	$\dfrac{dr}{d\bar{A}} = 0$	$\dfrac{dr}{d\bar{A}} > 0$	$\dfrac{dr}{d\bar{A}} = 0$	$\dfrac{dr}{d\bar{A}} > 0$
	$\dfrac{dY}{d\bar{A}} = 0$	$\dfrac{dY}{d\bar{A}} > 0$	$\dfrac{dY}{d\bar{A}} > 0$	$\dfrac{dY}{d\bar{A}} = 0$
	$\dfrac{de}{d\bar{A}} < 0$	$\dfrac{de}{d\bar{A}} > 0$	$\dfrac{de}{d\bar{A}} = 0$	$\dfrac{de}{d\bar{A}} = 0$
	$\dfrac{dT}{d\bar{A}} < 0$	$\dfrac{dT}{d\bar{A}} = 0$	$\dfrac{dT}{d\bar{A}} < 0$	$\dfrac{dT}{d\bar{A}} = 0$
Money supply increase	$\dfrac{dr}{dM^s} = 0$	$\dfrac{dr}{dM^s} < 0$	$\dfrac{dr}{dM^s} = 0$	$\dfrac{dr}{dM^s} = 0$
	$\dfrac{dY}{dM^s} > 0$	$\dfrac{dY}{dM^s} > 0$	$\dfrac{dY}{dM^s} = 0$	$\dfrac{dY}{dM^s} = 0$
	$\dfrac{de}{dM^s} > 0$	$\dfrac{de}{dM^s} > 0$	$\dfrac{de}{dM^s} = 0$	$\dfrac{de}{dM^s} = 0$
	$\dfrac{dT}{dM^s} > 0$	$\dfrac{dT}{dM^s} = 0$	$\dfrac{dT}{dM^s} = 0$	$\dfrac{dT}{dM^s} = 0$

is somewhat unrealistic for many small economies where tradable commodities are highly substitutable for foreign goods. In contrast, the model asymmetrically specifies that in financial markets, domestic and foreign bonds are perfect substitutes under the perfect capital mobility assumption, ignoring the possibility of international interest risk premia.

The simple Keynesian consumption function included in the basic model is of course subject to all the criticisms and alternative specifications such as the relative, permanent and life-cycle hypotheses expounded in the closed economy literature.[3] Likewise, the closed-economy literature includes alternative, more sophisticated investment functions, than that proposed in the standard MF model.[4] With respect to the impact of government spending and taxing on total expenditure, the MF model implies that activist fiscal policies can be easily implemented, irrespective of recognition and implementation lags.

Another unrealistic assumption of the basic MF model is that national price levels are fixed. This deficiency has however been addressed by some authors[5] who allow exchange rate changes to affect the price level and hence real balances with feedback effects on the real sector, thus modifying but not substantially changing the standard conclusions of the approach. Relatedly, the implicit assumption of the basic MF model that aggregate supply is perfectly elastic has been relaxed. For instance, Bruce and Purvis (1985) demonstrate that the standard policy ineffectiveness results are still valid only if nominal wages are rigid; otherwise with variable wages and a changing price level there are associated supply side effects which, with perfect capital mobility, can render monetary policy ineffective but make fiscal policy effective under floating rates. Despite recognising the need for a supply side and changing price level, these extended MF models continue, however, to constrain the output and expenditure aggregates of the national accounts to the same value, in and out of equilibrium, contrary to absorption related approaches.

6.4.2   External accounts specification

Moreover, the MF approach is founded on an *ad hoc* formulation of the external accounts. As expressed in equation (6.3) above, the trade account and capital flows are treated only partially and are not integrated with the rest of the national accounts through the flow of funds. A more specific shortcoming concerns the inconsistency between having a flow equilibrium condition for the capital account, which underlies the *BP* curve, and the stock equilibrium condition in the domestic money market, which underlies the *LM* curve. As well, the model neglects the possibility that rising external indebtedness may itself limit capital inflow, should foreign investors be averse to rising foreign debt levels.

In treating capital flows as purchases and sales of debt instruments, the MF model omits foreign purchases of equities (row 5 of Figure 2.4) or real assets such as property which can be a significant portion of total capital flows. Yet, foreign claims to real domestic assets can explain the process of real international capital transfer and economic growth as proposed later in Chapter 8.

The basic MF model also unrealistically assumes that exchange rate expectations are static. Dornbusch (1976) addresses this omission by allowing forward looking expectations about the exchange rate to drive a wedge between domestic and foreign interest rates through the uncovered interest parity condition. By allowing asset prices to adjust more quickly than goods prices, Dornbusch's MF foundations emphasise the stickiness of prices in goods markets, in order to model exchange rate overshooting, and hence provide an alternative to the monetary approach to exchange rate determination. The Dornbusch exchange rate model also distinguishes between short run and long run effects of monetary expansion in contrast to the short run adjustment focus of the earlier MF literature.

With respect to the specification of the external accounts in the MF model, a further deficiency on this score is its failure to recognise the often quantitatively significant income and transfers sub-account of the current account which arises because international financial flows require servicing through interest obligations, often payable immediately. In turn, growth in such payments widens the gap between national output and income according to national accounting principles. Nor is it recognised that changes in competitiveness arising from nominal exchange rate movements cause valuation effects for the current account of the kind discussed in Chapter 2. Relatedly, there are no J-curve effects because there are no export or import adjustment lags and the export and import demand elasticities are presumed to fulfil the Marshall–Lerner condition immediately, such that appreciations (depreciations) quickly lower (raise) net exports.

A final criticism of the MF approach is that it ignores the impact of foreign investment flows on the economy's total capital stock, in much the same way as closed economy Keynesian models neglect the impact of domestic investment flows on the domestic capital stock. In the closed economy case, allowing investment to matter for aggregate demand in the short run, but not matter for aggregate supply, has been justified on the grounds that the purchase of capital goods immediately increases aggregate demand, but not aggregate supply due to installation lags. Furthermore, it is argued, supply side effects can be ignored since annual investment spending is a more significant portion of expenditure than of the existing capital stock.

However, the supply side effects of investment are macroeconomically relevant if new capital equipment is quickly put to work.

Moreover, the suggestion that investment spending is insignificant relative to the value of the existing capital stock neglects that recently accumulated real capital can yield higher marginal productivity than preexisting capital if it embodies new technology. Aggregate supply will also fall in the absence of replacement capital which is usually recorded as a substantial part of gross investment flows in advanced economies.

6.5   Ricardian equivalence

As suggested by the MF model and the earlier loanable funds model of Chapter 4, the 'twin-deficits' hypothesis, ultimately depends on unchanged private saving behaviour in the face of increased fiscal deficits and rising public debt.[6] These alternative transmission mechanisms of these models are however subject to the ambiguities raised by the Ricardian equivalence (RE) theorem based on David Ricardo's proposition that tax and bond financing of government expenditure were equivalent in their effects on private consumption spending. Essentially, in generalised form the RE proposition is based on households' perceptions of government bonds held in their investment portfolios. An increase in bond holdings may not imply an increase in financial wealth, since bonds also represent the future obligation of the government which the private sector will ultimately have to meet through higher taxes. Hence, an increase in public debt outstanding as a result of higher budget deficits arising from either increased government spending or reduced taxes should therefore lead to higher private saving in preparation for the future tax burden. If private agents care as much about their descendants' economic welfare as their own, it does not even matter if the future taxes are not levied in their own lifetime.

This proposition in its strict form implies that the scope for active fiscal policy is non existent. Contrary to the traditional Keynesian approach, which asserts that individuals treat tax cuts like any other form of income, budgetary measures intended to stimulate private spending would be immediately offset by reduced spending as economic agents realise that fiscal expansion, budget deficits and higher public debt levels imply future tax increases. In terms of the *IS–LM–BP* diagram, the RE proposition suggests that government attempts to shift the *IS* curve prove futile, thus eliminating any link between the public and external accounts.

In terms of the saving-investment models, if RE held in a strict sense, there would likewise be no effect on the external imbalance because, with either increased public consumption or investment there would be an offsetting fall in private consumption at given levels of output. With increased public consumption widening the public account deficit, RE implies no net change in the position of the S^A schedule from the earlier Figure 4.6, whereas with increased public investment it implies that any rightward shift in the I^A schedule is matched by a rightward shift of the S^A schedule, leaving the external imbalance unchanged at the prevailing interest rate. In practice, only if RE does not hold on a one for one basis, would there be a link between domestic fiscal and external deficits.

Although the RE proposition in its strict form negates the 'twin-deficits' application of the MF model, reality suggests a link could exist in principle, because agents have incomplete information. Moreover, some agents may not expect future tax increases to apply to them personally and hence not adjust their behaviour. Furthermore, there is the possibility of reverse causality between the public and external accounts, contrary to the line of causality proposed by the 'twin-deficits' hypothesis. For example, in the event of a foreign financed private investment boom, the CAD would rise but, other things equal, the budget deficit would tend to surplus as tax revenue increased because of rising incomes.

Moreover, changes in taxes or public spending may, through incentive effects, alter private sector saving and investment behaviour in other ways. Hence, RE may be necessary but not sufficient for a one to one relationship between the consolidated public account and the external imbalance. There is also evidence that private and public saving are imperfect substitutes, contrary to the RE proposition, such that variations in the fiscal stance are likely to have affected external account outcomes by altering the pattern of public saving and investment.

Conceptual issues also arise as to whether a large part of public expenditure is more appropriately classified as investment rather than consumption. For instance, to the extent that increased health and education spending, now defined in national accounts as public consumption, improves the productivity of the human capital stock, it could be considered as contributing to increased public investment, rather than lower public saving. Though recent patterns of public saving and investment in advanced economies would look quite different if reclassified this way, *ceteris paribus*, the size of recorded foreign investment flows would nonetheless remain the same.

6.6 Conclusion

Although the MF model highlights the macroeconomic implications of international financial flows, it fails to embed these flows adequately into real macroeconomic relationships relating domestic and foreign investment, domestic capital accumulation, rates of return on real capital and national income. Nor does it make saving and investment decisions central to external account determination.

National accounting, however, dictates that net capital inflow over any period can only occur if there has been a corresponding change in the nation's saving–investment imbalance, and relative wealth levels, the principal determinants of which should be explained in any general equilibrium model with reference to common real factors. Hence the emphasis in MF genus models on capital flows as purely financial phenomena, not directly tied to real phenomena, or intertemporal forces is incomplete.

Financial capital flows recorded in the capital account are not independent of the process of real international capital transfer, yet the MF model fails to capture this. On the other hand, output and expenditure decisions can indeed be independent of each other, as stressed by the absorption approaches, yet the MF model implies the opposite. In defence of the MF model, it may of course be argued that it was never designed to explain external account determination, but instead provides a starting point for analysing short run responses in income and exchange rates.

It is the purpose of the next chapter to provide an alternative approach to analysing macroeconomic policy in the open economy. This framework addresses many of the basic deficiencies of the MF and earlier approaches outlined above.

7
Money, Expenditure and External Adjustment

This chapter develops an international monetary framework for analysing monetary and fiscal shocks that is consistent with open economy budget constraints and standard precepts of international finance. The framework is used to capture macroeconomic and financial activity under both fixed and floating exchange rates, explicitly tracing out the external adjustment process.

Previous chapters have expounded a range of international monetary models that can be dichotomised as either partial or macroeconomic in their coverage. That is, they have restricted attention to one or more select markets of the economy on the goods or financial side, as with the elasticities, purchasing power parity and conventional arbitrage-based interest parity approaches. Alternatively, they have combined open economy goods and financial markets in general equilibrium settings, incorporating national accounting aggregates and employment. The matrix of Table 7.1 provides a basic taxonomy of existing international monetary models along such lines.

The model presented in what follows is macroeconomic, but in states of equilibrium is also fully consistent with the partial parity conditions. It differs from other economy-wide approaches in numerous ways. For instance, the earlier monetary approach to the balance of payments and exchange rate put monetary and price level linkages at the centre of the analysis of external adjustment. Yet, it failed to account satisfactorily for the interaction between national production, spending, the domestic monetary sector, interest rates and the international flow of funds. Meanwhile, exchange rate and price level effects were

Table 7.1   Taxonomy of international monetary models

Coverage / Variable	Partial	Macroeconomic
Current account, Balance of payments	Elasticities	Monetary, Intertemporal, Mundell–Fleming
Exchange rate, Interest rates, Price levels	Interest parity, Purchasing power parity, Portfolio balance	Monetary, Mundell–Fleming
Income, Employment	—	Intertemporal, Mundell–Fleming

neglected in the Fisherian intertemporal set-up founded on divergent national saving and investment behaviour.

Over recent decades exchange rate economics has been dominated by asset market models, which emphasise stock rather than flow relations. The monetary approach to the exchange rate for instance, is based on the relative money stock holdings of residents and foreigners, whereas the portfolio balance approach presumes the exchange rate is capital account determined, though some variants include current account feedback effects on asset stocks. These stock oriented asset market approaches have not, however, found strong empirical support.

Meanwhile, the capital side of the external accounts implicitly dominates the behaviour of the exchange rate in the floating rate version of the Mundell–Fleming model of the last chapter, while capital account balances are treated as measures of a nation's net international borrowing requirement in intertemporal models of external adjustment. The emphasis in international monetary theory on asset markets and capital account transactions as primary influences on the nominal exchange rate contrasts with the flow approach in which the exchange rate simultaneously equalised net demand and supply of foreign currency arising from both current and capital account transactions.

The continued popularity of Mundell–Fleming (MF) framework undoubtedly stems from its clear prescriptions for macroeconomic policy, its broad coverage of economy-wide variables and its capacity to interrelate key variables graphically. However, as stressed in the extensive critique of the previous chapter, its usefulness is limited by numerous specification problems. In contrast, this chapter proposes an alternative transmission mechanism for macroeconomic policy in an open economy that links national output, expenditure, the exchange rate, international financial flows, the current account, employment and the price level. Moreover, unlike other international monetary models, it illustrates the external adjustment process under circumstances where foreign investors react to an open economy's evolving macroeconomic fundamentals.

7.1 An open economy AD/AS framework

7.1.1 Underlying relationships

This section develops the underlying linkages subsequently used to model monetary and fiscal shocks on key international macroeconomic variables. The basic national accounting relations of the model are

$$C_p + I_p + C_g + I_g = A \tag{7.1}$$

$$A - Y = CAD = FI \tag{7.2}$$

In equation (7.1), C_p is private consumption, I_p is private investment, C_g is public consumption, I_g is public investment and A is total absorption, or aggregate demand, all in real flow terms. Equation (7.2) shows that the absolute difference between national expenditure and national output, Y, or aggregate supply, is equivalent to the initial trade (current account) deficit, CAD, which, *ex post*, must also equal capital inflow, FI, and the rise in the stock of external liabilities, over the same period. Hence, foreigners acquire increased holdings of domestically issued financial instruments whenever aggregate demand exceeds aggregate supply or residents acquire increased holdings of foreign issued financial instruments whenever aggregate supply exceeds aggregate demand, *ex post*.

A necessary condition for equation (7.2) to hold is that the net demand for foreign currency arising from the difference between national spending and output is matched by a corresponding net supply of foreign currency associated with the capital inflow. As a corollary, it follows that if official restrictions prohibit international capital flows such that capital immobility prevails, then any *ex ante* gap between spending and output is eliminated through exchange rate adjustment. If the exchange rate is fixed, the gap is closed through a change in the foreign exchange reserves of the central bank.

In this model, it is assumed that all goods and services are internationally tradable. Hence, in final equilibrium the domestic price level is simply the product of an exogenous world price (P^*) and the nominal effective exchange rate (e), defined as the trade weighted price of foreign exchange, $P = eP^*$. It is also possible to imagine a two country version with an invariant foreign price level. By setting the foreign price level at unity,

$$P = e, \text{ as a long-run equilibrium condition} \qquad (7.3)$$

The domestic money stock (M^s) is determined by the home economy's central bank. Equilibrium in the domestic money market occurs when residents' real demand for cash balances (L), which is negatively related to the domestic interest rate (r) and positively related to the level of real wealth (W), equals the real supply of money. That is,

$$M^s/P = L(r; W) \quad L_r < 0, L_w > 0 \qquad (7.4)$$

It follows from both equations (7.3) and (7.4) that the stronger the exchange rate, the lower is the price level, the larger is the real money stock and, for given domestic money demand and nominal money supply, the lower is the real interest rate, as shown in Figure 7.1.

7.1.2 Aggregate demand and supply functions

Aggregate demand is comprised of consumption and investment expenditure. Private consumption is negatively related to the exchange rate, the price level and the real interest rate, but positively related to national income. Private investment is also negatively related to the exchange rate, the price level and the real interest rate. Autonomous changes in public consumption and public investment are shift factors. Hence, in summary,

$$A = A\,(r(e, P); M^s, L, C_g, I_g) \qquad (7.5)$$
$$A_r < 0, A_e < 0, A_p < 0, A_{M^s} > 0$$
$$A_L < 0, A_{C_g} > 0, A_{I_g} > 0$$

Equation (7.5) now provides the basis for an *AD* schedule in price level – expenditure and income space, as shown in Figure 7.2.

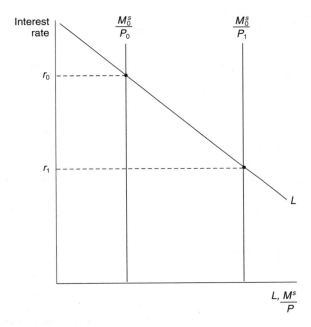

Figure 7.1   Money market equilibrium

The economic rationale for its negative slope is that, other things equal, a stronger exchange rate (lower price level) increases the real money supply, which lowers the real domestic interest rate, thereby inducing higher private consumption and investment spending. Alternatively, the negative slope of the AD schedule can be rationalised on the basis that a lower price level raises the economy's real wealth level, which induces higher expenditure for given real income. Since the AD schedule is drawn for a given nominal money supply and real money demand, money supply or demand disturbances are also shift factors.

Turning to the aggregate supply side of the economy, this can be represented with reference to a standard macroeconomic production function. Here again, it is assumed that the total domestic output of

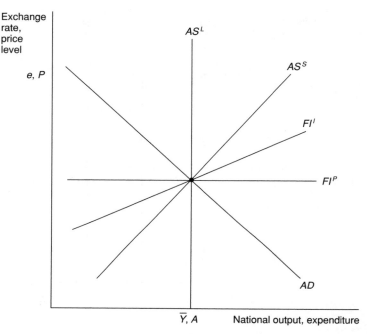

Figure 7.2   Open economy analytical framework

goods and services provided for sale to residents and foreigners depends on the use of the available factor inputs – labour, l, the economy's tangible capital stock, K, and technology, τ. Hence

$$Y = Y(l, K, \tau) \quad Y_l > 0, Y_K > 0, Y_\tau > 0 \tag{7.6}$$

In the long run, all domestic prices including wages are presumed fully flexible, such that the goods and services markets clear and unemployment is at the natural rate. Hence, the aggregate supply schedule is vertical above $\overline{Y}$, as shown in Figure 7.2. In the short run, however, wages and product prices may be sticky because of fixed-term contracts. Moreover, if export contracts are denominated in local currency, firms would find that foreign demand for their product increases (decreases) on relative price grounds following nominal depreciations (appreciations) until full pass-through has occurred. This contrasts with the more immediate pass through of exchange rate changes on the expenditure side via imports which are invariably denominated in foreign currency. These rigidities allow the real wage and real exchange rate to change, thus affecting the international competitiveness of domestic firms.

In general, the behaviour of output in the short run can be summarised by the equation

$$Y = \overline{Y} + \sigma(eP^* - P) \tag{7.7}$$

where σ is an adjustment parameter.

This equation shows for instance that if exports are priced below the world price for the above-mentioned reasons, then national output can rise above its normal level. Hence, equation (7.7) also conveys that real appreciations (depreciations) temporarily lower (raise) output above its normal level. Accordingly, short run aggregate supply behaves as depicted by the AS^s schedule in Figure 7.2.

7.1.3 International investment flows

To complete the framework, it is necessary to incorporate the key international financial relations which link transnational capital flows to the domestic interest rate, the foreign interest rate and to exchange rate expectations. Here it is assumed foreigners consider investing in domestic currency denominated debt instruments issued by resident entities on the basis of both relative interest returns and anticipated exchange rate movement over the term of holding such instruments. In net terms, any inflow of foreign exchange to finance an excess of national expenditure over national output is measured as the capital account surplus in the nation's external accounts. Outflows of domestic funds arising from aggregate output rising above aggregate expenditure are reflected in capital account deficits.

Stock equilibrium for the capital account prevails when the uncovered interest parity condition is met, such that

$$r + \hat{a} = r^* \tag{7.8}$$

where $\hat{a}$ is the appreciation of the domestic currency expected by foreigners and r^* is the exogenous foreign interest rate, all over a given time period.

For equation (7.8) to hold, domestic and foreign financial assets must be deemed fully substitutable by foreign investors. Yet, foreigners are likely to think that investing funds in a particular economy becomes more risky the higher the current account deficit and the higher the level of foreign debt. Accordingly, foreign investors will demand extra compensation to fund an expenditure-output gap through an interest risk premium, ρ, where $\rho \geq 0$. The higher is the value of ρ, the less mobile is international capital, with the limit value of $\rho = 0$ corresponding to the extreme of perfect capital mobility.

Whenever international capital is less than perfectly mobile, the equilibrium condition therefore becomes $r + \hat{a} - \rho = r^*$. In flow terms, it is possible to state that

$$FI = FI(\rho; r, \hat{a}, r^*) \quad FI_\rho < O, FI_r > O, FI_{\hat{a}} > O, FI_{r^*} < O \tag{7.9}$$

where FI is the quantum of foreign currency which flows into the host economy to acquire domestic currency denominated debt instruments.

A third schedule which captures international financial equilibrium, labelled the FI schedule, can now be added to the AD/AS framework. This schedule is horizontal, as shown in Figure 7.2 if capital mobility is perfect, upward sloping if imperfect and vertical if completely immobile. As suggested by equation (7.9), domestic interest rate rises and expected exchange rate appreciations shift the FI schedule downwards, whereas foreign interest rate rises shift it upwards. Heightened risk associated with international investment steepens the slope of the FI schedule.

In this framework, the economy is in general equilibrium at the point of intersection between the AD, AS and FI schedules. If capital mobility is perfect and if the future exchange rate is expected to be the same as its present value, then real domestic and foreign interest rates will also initially be equal at this point.

7.2 Monetary shocks

It is now possible to examine the effectiveness of monetary policy under fixed and floating exchange rates. In what follows, the analysis assumes capital mobility is not perfect and hence employs an upward sloping FI^p schedule.

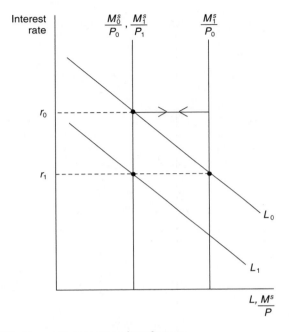

Figure 7.3   Domestic monetary disturbances

7.2.1   Monetary expansion under fixed exchange rate

Consider first the economy-wide impact of a monetary expansion which results from a central bank open market purchase of bonds from residents. An exogenous rise in the nominal money supply from M_0^s to M_1^s initially lowers domestic interest rates from r_0 to r_1 as shown in Figure 7.3.

The lower domestic interest rate thereby induces greater consumption and investment expenditure by resident households and firms, shifting the *AD* curve rightward as shown in Figure 7.4. The higher domestic expenditure in excess of national output thereby tends to generate a current account deficit, as measured by the horizontal

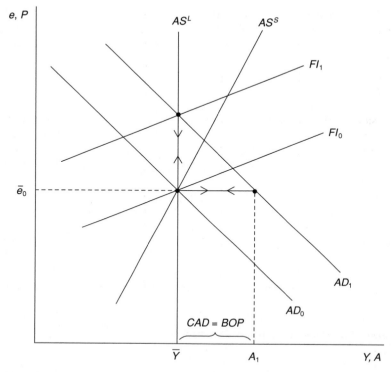

Figure 7.4   Monetary expansion under fixed exchange rate

distance between AD_0 and AD_1. Since the domestic real interest rate temporarily falls relative to the foreign interest rate, foreigners would be unwilling to finance any current account deficit arising from increased domestic spending over output at exchange rate e_0. The FI_0 schedule therefore immediately shifts upward to FI_I as relative interest rates favour outward investment.

To maintain the exchange rate at $\bar{e}_0$, the monetary authorities must purchase domestic currency in the foreign exchange market using accumulated foreign reserves. This manifests as a temporary balance of payments deficit equivalent to the current account deficit. If left unsterilised, this foreign exchange market intervention necessarily offsets the original money supply increase. Accordingly, the domestic interest rate reverts to its original level in Figure 7.3 and the *AD* curve returns to its starting point in Figure 7.4. As domestic and foreign interest rates equalise, the *FI* schedule also returns to its original position. Hence monetary expansion is impossible given the exchange rate constraint, though of course the composition of the central bank's balance sheet changes *ex post*.

If the source of monetary disturbance in Figure 7.3 was a fall in residents' demand for money from L_0 to L_1 rather than an exogenous increase, then this would also act to lower the domestic interest rate, shifting the *AD* curve rightward, generating an excess demand for foreign currency. Under these circumstances, the central bank then has to reduce the domestic money supply to the same extent as the fall in money demand to maintain the value of the exchange rate at $\bar{e}_0$.

It follows from this framework that sterilised foreign exchange market intervention by the central bank in the wake of expansionary open market operations would be completely ineffective as a means of preventing exchange rate depreciation. This is because sterilised intervention would not reverse the extra domestic expenditure due to the initial money supply increase and fall in domestic interest rates.

7.2.2 Monetary expansion under floating exchange rate

Under a floating exchange rate (Figure 7.5), forward looking foreign investors judge that a lower interest rate and increased domestic spending must eventually depreciate the nominal exchange rate as a result of monetary expansion. Hence, the FI_0 schedule again immediately rises to FI_0. Because the incipient current account deficit attributable to the higher expenditure would remain unfinanced, the exchange rate then actually depreciates from e_0 to e_1, the domestic real interest rate rises and residents' expenditure falls with movement up along the AD_1 schedule.

A current account surplus, CAS_1, temporarily arises to the extent that improved competitiveness raises domestic output to Y_1 in the short run as production moves up along the AS_1^s schedule. However, as nominal wages are bid up to restore real wages and as export prices fully adjust, the AS^s schedule drifts up toward the final equilibrium.

Note, however, that as the nominal exchange rate depreciates and the domestic price level rises, the real money supply also begins to fall. Eventually, the real money supply schedule is restored to its initial level $\left(\dfrac{M_0^s}{e_o} = \dfrac{M_1^s}{e_1} \right)$ such that the real interest rate again equals its initial

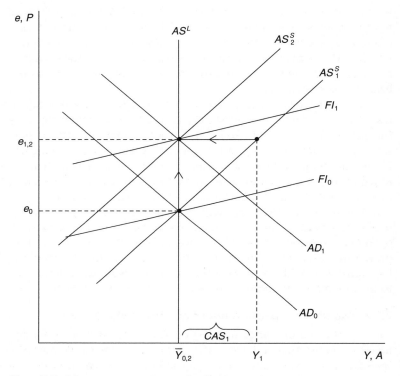

Figure 7.5   Monetary expansion under floating exchange rate

equilibrium value. At the same time, the nominal interest rate would have risen to the extent of the nominal depreciation and the inflation that was generated. Hence in this model, expansionary monetary policy only temporarily influences expenditure and output through its effect on the real interest rate and competitiveness, though permanently changes the price level, consistent with the long run neutrality proposition.

7.2.3   Foreign interest rate shock

If the world interest rate rises, then as shown in Figure 7.6 there is an upward shift in the FI_0 schedule to FI_1. Residents would tend to reduce their holdings of cash balances and increase their investment abroad.

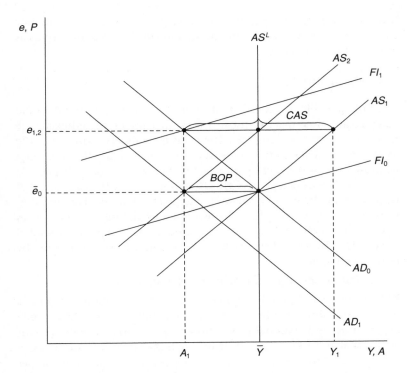

Figure 7.6   A rise in the foreign interest rate

However, to prevent this capital outflow from depreciating the exchange rate under circumstances where the exchange rate is fixed, the central bank must buy the excess supply of domestic currency in the foreign exchange market, thus depleting its foreign reserves. This contraction of the domestic money supply thereby raises domestic interest rates to the world level which in turn reduces domestic expenditure and shifts the AD_0 schedule inward to AD_1. The extent of this shift is then also a measure of the current account surplus that arises as domestic expenditure contracts at the given exchange rate, $\bar{e}_0$.

Alternatively, if the exchange rate floats, no offsetting monetary contraction occurs. Residents reduce holdings of domestic money balances and invest in foreign bonds creating an excess demand for foreign currency. Hence, the economy experiences a currency depreciation, temporary rise in output and current account surplus as well as a higher price level.

7.3   Fiscal shocks

It is now possible to use this framework to analyse the international macroeconomic impact of fiscal shocks, first under a fixed exchange rate, then under a floating rate. The focus is on fiscal expansion in the form of public expenditure increases, since interpreting the economy-wide effects of discretionary income tax changes is more complicated due to possible work incentive effects on households. It is assumed that the rises in public spending are not matched by domestic tax increases, so that in each case explored below, a domestic budget deficit arises that is funded through the issue of domestic currency denominated bonds. The analysis abstracts from Ricardian effects covered in the previous chapter.

7.3.1   Public spending under fixed exchange rate

With reference to Figure 7.7, a hike in government spending augments national spending, shifting the *AD* schedule right. The excess national expenditure over national production gives rise to a current account deficit that must be financed. If international investors are to some extent averse to rising external imbalances, the *FI* schedule slopes upward. Hence, there will be pressure on the exchange rate to depreciate, so the central bank has to meet the financing requirement by running down its official reserve assets, selling foreign currency in exchange for domestic currency. The central bank thereby contracts the domestic money supply, raising the real domestic interest rate in the process. This reverses the initial shift in the *AD* curve.

Any rise in the fiscal deficit due to increased public expenditure therefore only causes a temporary rise in the current account deficit. External equilibrium is eventually restored, but at the cost of a depletion of the central bank's foreign exchange reserves. The price level is unaffected throughout the adjustment process while employment levels remain unchanged to the extent that employment is related more to production than expenditure. This framework thus yields a result that is contrary to standard MF analysis by showing that public expenditure increases are an ineffective way of raising national income under a fixed exchange rate.

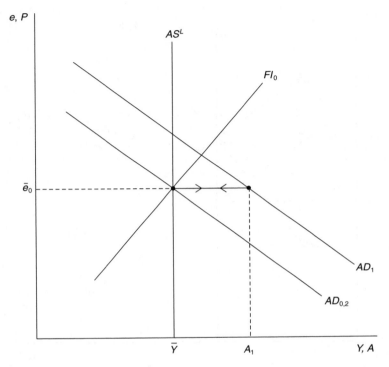

Figure 7.7 Higher public spending under fixed exchange rate

7.3.2 Public spending under floating exchange rate

Next consider the effects of public expenditure increases under a floating rate. Under these conditions, the forward-looking expectations of foreign investors become central to external adjustment in the manner they were for understanding exchange rate behaviour in the extended intertemporal model of Chapter 5. Again, foreign investors' reactions to expenditure shocks in an open economy depend on their views about the use to which borrowed funds are put. In particular, it is critical whether international financial inflows finance extra public consumption or extra public investment in the host economy.

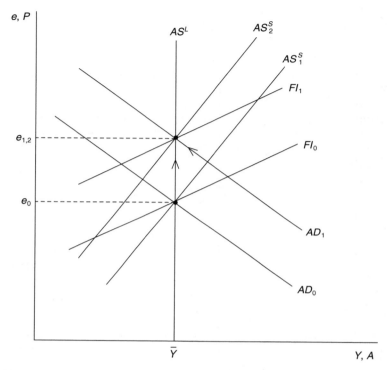

Figure 7.8   Higher public consumption under floating exchange rate

Public consumption

First consider the case of an increase in public consumption. As domestic private and prior public spending is supplemented, the AD schedule of Figure 7.8 shifts right, inducing a current account deficit as shown. However, as higher public consumption will not add to future national production, but to future net demand for foreign currency when foreign loans mature, a later currency depreciation becomes inevitable. The FI schedule therefore shifts up to FI and the nominal exchange rate immediately depreciates from e_0 to e_1. The domestic real interest rate rises simultaneously and total domestic expenditure is choked off as the economy moves up along the AD curve.

As was the case with pure monetary expansion under a floating exchange rate, a current account surplus may temporarily emerge in the short run as competitiveness improves and short run output rises along *AS*. Again however, export prices will adjust and nominal domestic wages will eventually be bid up to maintain workers' domestic purchasing power. These factors combine to push the short-run *AS* schedule up without any long-run change in real national income. Consequently, fiscal expansion of this kind proves ineffective as a lasting means of boosting national income, although it permanently raises the domestic price level.

Interestingly however, it has also been shown that fiscal expansion (contraction) weakens (strengthens) the economy's exchange rate, contrary to the popular Mundell–Fleming model. As it turns out, this fiscal-exchange rate linkage is more consistent with empirical evidence on the relationship between fiscal shocks and exchange rate behaviour. For instance, according to an International Monetary Fund (1996) study of episodes of fiscal consolidation since the 1980s in Australia, Belgium, Denmark, Ireland, Japan, New Zealand, Norway, Sweden and the United States, nominal and real exchange rates tended to appreciate rather than depreciate following sustained reductions in public expenditure.

Public investment

Finally, it remains to consider the international macroeconomic effects and external adjustment process of an increase in public investment, empirically a relatively small proportion of public spending in most economies. As with higher public consumption, higher public investment initially shifts the *AD* schedule out and generates a current account deficit, as depicted in Figure 7.9.

The difference here is that foreign investors should be willing to fund the current account deficit if the higher public investment is expected to increase the size and overall productivity of the economy's capital stock. For if so, aggregate output can be expected to increase in the future, consistent with the intertemporal approach outlined in earlier chapters. If the rise in aggregate output is expected to at least cover higher subsequent expenditure and demand for foreign currency, this suggests the current account deficit that emerges is sustainable in the sense that there is no immediate depreciation to eliminate it.

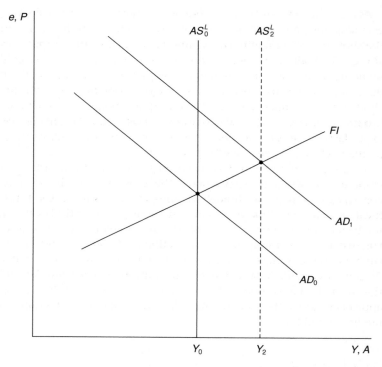

Figure 7.9   Higher public investment under floating exchange rate

The actual size of the deficit in the first instance is governed by the degree of international capital mobility and hence the slope of the *FI* schedule. The higher is the degree of capital mobility, the larger is the current account deficit and the smaller is the exchange rate depreciation and rise in inflation following fiscal expansion in this form. Of course, Ricardian effects are still possible in the wake of public spending rises. In the extreme, though empirically unsupported case, a one for one offset of private consumption by resident households mindful of future tax obligations would always prevent an output–expenditure gap arising in the first instance.

Furthermore, with asymmetric information as modelled earlier in Chapter 5 international investors' expectations may change if perceived country risk levels suddenly rise, or if expectations about the future output generating capacity of the economy are revised. This would lead to an immediate upward shift of the *FI* schedule that may precipitate a currency crisis of the sort discussed later in Chapter 9.

7.4   Summary and implications

Just how monetary and fiscal policy affect economy wide variables has been the subject of extensive theorising over a long period of time. Unfortunately, existing frameworks provide an incomplete account of the transmission mechanism of macroeconomic policy in open economies. In particular, earlier approaches neglect the fact that international investors may react instantly to the prospect of higher external deficits they perceive to be unsustainable, with the result that significant exchange rate depreciations may occur. They also neglect that exchange rate depreciations may be a major source of inflationary pressures in increasingly open economies.

The model outlined above provides an alternative means of analysing the transmission of monetary and fiscal policy in an open economy. Unlike models outlined in previous chapters, it explicitly identifies how an open economy's spending, output, external accounts, exchange rate, interest rate, employment and price level adjust when international capital is highly mobile and domestic and foreign agents are forward looking.

It suggests that under a floating exchange rate regime, monetary shocks can affect national output and expenditure quite differently, with implications for the behaviour of employment and current account balances in the short run, as well as the economy's price level in the longer run. It shows that monetary expansion under fixed rates generates temporary external deficits without output or inflationary consequences. Whereas under floating rates, monetary expansion depreciates the nominal and real exchange rates, lifting output and employment temporarily in the short run but raising the domestic price level in the long run.

Fiscal expansion under a fixed exchange rate in the form of higher public spending is shown to have similar effects to a money supply increase under a fixed rate. However, under a floating rate the nature of the public spending increase and how international investors react to it is pivotal to external adjustment. Higher public consumption can depreciate the exchange rate and raise the price level, thus yielding macroeconomic outcomes similar to a domestic monetary expansion under a floating rate. On the other hand, higher public investment can permanently raise national output without severe inflationary consequences if capital mobility is high and the government spending is productive.

This alternative framework also yields results that are relevant to the long-running international economic policy debate about exchange rate choice. It implies that fixed exchange rates prevent monetary disturbances from affecting real output and employment, even though real expenditure and current account imbalances may rise or fall as a result. It also suggests that economies prone to high inflation may be better served by a fixed exchange rate regime such as a currency board system, provided world inflation is low.

8
Foreign Capital and Economic Growth

This chapter focuses mainly on the nexus between international capital movements and long-run economic growth in open economies. The exposition emphasises real capital mobility to show how capital account balances may be determined over the longer term through an arbitrage process which tends to equalise the productivity of foreign financed capital and its international rental cost. It then models the transitional dynamics of international capital account adjustment for external deficit economies in response to world interest rate shocks and endogenous changes in the tax treatment of foreign versus domestic capital. It also considers the behaviour of financial claims to capital and the dynamics of economic growth for capital importing economies, before drawing conclusions about the policy significance of international capital movements.

8.1 Saving, investment and capital flows

Earlier chapters suggested that international capital flows could be explained in terms of the difference between domestic saving and investment. This, for instance, made it possible to examine how, for given national income levels, international interest differentials arose. Yet, the intertemporal approach also showed that changes in saving, investment and financial flows themselves affect national output and income. Figure 8.1 conveys this in another way. Domestic saving is depicted in this diagram as an increasing function of output and hence national disposable income, whereas investment opportunities are presumed autonomous. All variables are expressed in real terms.

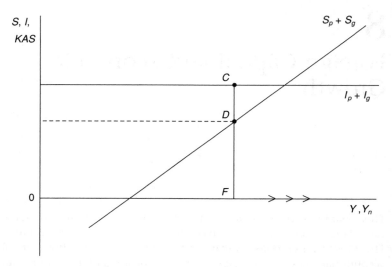

Figure 8.1   Saving, investment and the external accounts

Contrary to the closed economy case where the level of national saving fully constrains investment spending, this framework again shows that in an open economy, domestic investment, both private and public, may be independent of domestic saving. The difference between ex ante investment and saving determines the current and capital account balances at any level of output. Unlike the loanable funds approach of Chapters 4 and 5, it explicitly allows for changing national income levels and contrary to the MF model of Chapter 6, it is consistent with the absorption approach, since changes in domestic expenditure at given output levels immediately affect the external imbalance. Although saving is shown as an increasing function of income, the S schedule need not necessarily depict a simple Keynesian saving function, as usually assumed in the MF approach for example. If, for example, the horizontal axis was relabelled permanent income, the S schedule would still be upward sloping, but would pass through the origin.

Without foreign investment, domestic capital accumulation would be only *DF*. With foreign investment however, capital accumulation is that much greater and as real capital, net of depreciation, is an input to the production process, this extra capital should further increase the future level of output, a result consistent with the intertemporal approach of Chapter 4. The arrows on the horizontal axis of Figure 8.1 signify that the additional productive capital, which foreign investment permits, is being accumulated in an economy growing through time. Hence, this simple model abstracts from the business cycle and is best suited to demonstrating the external account consequences of medium to longer-run changes in saving and investment.

In countries where there had been significant financial liberalisation, the household saving component of total saving declined significantly however in the 1980s and 1990s. However, these falls in household saving tended to be offset by rises in business saving, leaving gross private saving, the aggregate of most interest from an international macroeconomic perspective, largely unchanged. Furthermore, the empirical evidence suggests that neither movements in interest rates nor the strong rise in private sector wealth in OECD countries had any effect on short run saving behaviour.

In economic policy circles, it is often suggested that external deficits of countries like the United States, Canada and Australia are a manifestation of domestic saving being 'too low'. Hence, by implication, policy measures should aim at shifting the saving schedule of Figure 8.1 upward to narrow the perceived problem of the external imbalance being 'too high'. But is such thinking misplaced in light of the fundamental determinants of domestic saving behaviour?

For example, demographic factors may be an important influence on saving patterns through time, both across countries and within countries. If the age composition of the population changes, so too will saving, insofar as consumption behaviour differs between different age groups. Consider the case of a nation which experiences a fall in the proportion of the population of working age and an associated rise in the proportion of retirees. If retirees have a higher consumption to income ratio, then consistent with the 'life-cycle' hypothesis, this could result in some fall in private saving, causing a downward shift of the S schedule of Figure 8.1.

Another demographic factor which could conceivably affect both domestic saving and investment behaviour is immigration, to the extent that it increases population growth, alters consumption patterns and creates a demand for additional capital to accommodate and employ the extra population. Significant differences in age profiles, combined with the nature of the social security system and the way it provides for retirement, are likely to account for at least part of the difference between saving rates across countries.

For instance, many advanced economies have generous publicly funded pension schemes, yet Japan, for example, does not. Hence, the high rate of Japanese saving over the 1990s may have been partly determined by the forward looking consumption behaviour of a significant component of its population. Japan has been a major source of capital inflow for many nations, and to the extent that demographic factors raised Japan's saving, it was an exogenous determinant of other nations' external imbalances. That is, increased capital outflow from Japan meant more domestic investment opportunities were exploited by domestic firms in other nations either borrowing part of this 'excess' foreign saving or by Japanese firms investing directly. With reference to Figure 8.1, total foreign investment and the investment schedule in host countries rose simultaneously.

Microeconomic distortions, due for instance to the nature of a nation's taxation system, may also make domestic saving less than optimal. The same may be said of tax systems abroad which make saving more than optimal. A fundamental determinant of private domestic investment is corporate profitability, a direct indicator of which is the ratio of gross operating surplus to the capital stock, that is GOS/K, an average measure. A higher profit share, to the extent it raises the rate of return on capital may give rise to an adjustment period characterised by buoyant investment and output growth. As an *ex post* average measure of the rate of return on capital GOS/K is, however, an imperfect proxy for the relative *ex ante* marginal rate concept used in the open economy capital theory to follow. Desirably, other macroeconomic rates of return on capital, such as relative earnings–price ratios for equities across country borders, should also be considered, but data limitations often prevent this.

Sustained increases in profitability can improve the ratio of the market valuation of companies to the replacement cost of capital. According to the 'q' theory of investment outlined later in this chapter, rises in q should of themselves stimulate additional real investment and therefore induce real capital transfer from abroad. In sum then, unexploited investment opportunities may initially be reflected in rising q values for companies listed on domestic stock exchanges. If so, in terms of our Figure 8.1, this suggests an economy's investment schedule would shift upward and as long as the additional investment is willingly financed by foreigners, it manifests as higher foreign investment.

Foreign saving may be borrowed by either domestic, or foreign controlled, firms to finance additional investment in host countries; this is essentially the portfolio versus direct foreign investment distinction defined in Chapter 2. Though foreign direct investment entails loss of control of corporate assets, it usually generates important benefits including technology transfer, international management expertise and product innovation.

With direct investment, the investment and funding decisions are often made simultaneously by multinational corporations. Therefore, increased imports of capital goods, recorded on the trade account may be matched at the same time by financial capital inflow to directly finance their purchase, though of course this will not necessarily occur. If it does, the extra supply of foreign exchange can therefore be used directly to purchase additional imported capital goods; hence, under these circumstances there is unlikely to be any effect on the exchange rate attributable to a change in the net flow demand for foreign currency.

8.2 Foreign capital as a source of growth

In the macroeconomics literature, the aggregate demand orientation of short-run Keynesian models is usually contrasted with long run growth models, which emphasise the aggregate supply side of the economy. Yet, as a rule, the modern growth literature still unrealistically neglects the impact of international resource flows.To improve understanding of the real significance of international capital flows, this section proposes an open economy growth accounting framework which identifies foreign investment and net capital inflow as a potential source of national output growth.

Standard growth accounting analysis following Solow (1956) suggests it is necessary to explore the role of the main factor inputs to production in the economy to appreciate the main causes of long-term economic performance. Traditionally, these factor inputs have been taken as the domestic labour force or hours worked, the economy's capital stock and the pace of technological advance. Mankiw, Romer and Weil (1992) have also shown that separately identifying human capital markedly reduces the empirical measure of our ignorance about the growth process. What this chapter suggests is that yet another distinction is appropriate for open economies within the traditional growth accounting framework. This distinction is that between domestically funded and foreign funded capital accumulation.

Consider a supply-side model of an open economy whose real capital stock comprises capital which has been accumulated through domestic saving and capital which has been accumulated through the use of foreign saving. In an open economy, total output or the aggregate supply of goods and services is determined by a macroeconomic production function, as for the closed economy case. However, in an open economy the macroeconomic production function may be specified differently as $Y = \Gamma f(K, K^*, l)$, where Y is national output or GDP, Γ is a technology parameter representing disembodied technical change, K is domestically funded capital accumulation, K^* is foreign investment and l is labour hours worked. The domestic labour force can also grow in this specification, but there is no immigration, since the focus remains international capital movements. For the same reason, human capital accumulation is not separately identified.

By differentiating this open economy production function, the sources of increased gross domestic product (Y) are revealed as

$$dY = f(K, K^*, l)d\Gamma + f_K dK + f_{K^*} dK^* + f_L dl \qquad (8.1)$$

where $f_{K,K^*,l}$ denotes the derivative of Y with respect to K, K^*, l.

For open economies, however, national output and national disposable income diverge to the extent of net income paid abroad. Hence

$$Y_n = Y - r^*(K^*).K^*$$

where Y_n is national disposable income and r^* is the interest cost on the use of foreign funded capital.

Therefore $dY_n = dY - (r^* dK^* + r_{K^*} K^* dK^*)$. If the country is small, it faces a perfectly elastic supply of foreign capital, so that the term $r_{K^*} K^* dK^*$ is zero. Hence

$$dY_n = dY - r^*dK^* \tag{8.2}$$

From (8.1) and (8.2), domestic and foreign sources of income growth can therefore be shown as

$$dY_n = \underbrace{f(K, K^*, l)d\Gamma + f_L dl + f_K dK}_{\text{domestic sources}} + \underbrace{f_{K^*} dK^* - r^* dK^*}_{\text{foreign source}} \tag{8.3}$$

The final bracketed term isolates the net contribution of foreign capital to growth in national income between states of long run equilibrium. The dynamic real welfare gains attributable to foreign investment may be estimated as $(f_{K^*} - r^*)dK^*$, where dK^* represents net foreign investment or the real capital account surplus.

The rental or user cost of capital is, of course, not only determined by the (domestic) interest rate faced by profit maximising firms, but also by the rate of capital consumption or depreciation because funds have to be spent maintaining plant and equipment in prime working condition. Abstracting from changing exchange rate expectations, the world interest rate is by definition the relevant interest rate which local firms face. Hence, the total rental cost of domestically funded capital is the same as the rental cost of foreign funded capital, inclusive of a given depreciation rate.

If capital consumption is introduced at a given rate of δ, then a sufficient condition for regarding the increased foreign investment positively is that $(f_{K^*} - \delta) > r^*$. In steady-state equilibrium the net marginal product of foreign capital used domestically would tend to equal the world interest rate. With only one transnational rate of return on capital, foreign capital would therefore cease to produce further domestic output in a direct way.

In sum, foreign investment transitionally increases an open economy's national income as long as the domestic return on foreign funded capital exceeds the rental cost of foreign capital. Of course, if technology was embodied in imported real foreign capital, as it may well be for small technology-dependent economies, there would be even higher transitional national income gains. Such foreign sourced technical gains would be captured within the traditional 'Solow residual'.

8.3   Graphical analysis

An analytical approach to the open economy that stressed the supply side to explain the real macroeconomic effects of foreign investment from abroad on a host economy first emerged in the 1960s.[1] It was based on neo-classical assumptions, including perfect competition in goods and factor markets, full employment, and no external economies in production. As well, it often assumed constant returns to scale.[2] Yet, it was never intended to explain how the external accounts as such were actually determined; indeed originally there was no explicit mention of current account or capital account imbalances.

8.3.1   The basic model

Consider an economy whose physical capital stock is small relative to the rest of the world's. In isolation, the economy's total gross output (Y) or aggregate supply of goods and services is determined by the simplest of macroeconomic production functions, $Y = f(K,L)$, where K is the gross value of the capital stock and L is labour effort. Only real capital is free to move internationally, which permits abstraction from the economics of labour migration. It is also assumed that the domestic labour force does not grow during the period of analysis.

Under competitive conditions in a closed economy whose initial capital stock is entirely owned by domestic residents, where the labour and goods markets clear instantly and where all output supplied by firms is demanded, the return to capital will equal its marginal product. Note that $f_k = \partial Y/\partial K > 0$ and $f_{kk} < 0$ by assumption. Initial output equilibrium would therefore be OD in Figure 8.2 where the slope of the production function reveals the marginal return on capital.[3] Aggregate gross income earned by capital is $f_k K$, as shown by distance AD.

Now if the foreign rate of return on capital (r^*) is lower than f_k, foreign investment (K^*) will eventually lead to an increase in the domestic capital stock to K_T, where $K_T = K + K^*$. Hence gross national output can be higher with foreign investment compared with autarky. B'C is paid to non-residents, so gross national income rises by CD'.

The basic model outlined above may now be extended by relaxing the assumption about an exogenous world interest rate. Consider, for instance, the case where, through foreign investment, one economic region is large enough to exert some influence on the productivity of

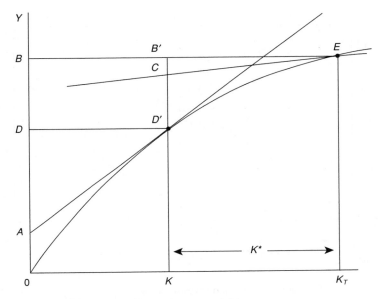

Figure 8.2   The gains from foreign investment (a)

capital, output and income in the other. Assume the two regions simultaneously move from autarky and permit foreign investment. They have similar production functions as depicted in Figure 8.3 and the combined capital stock is shown by the length of the horizontal axis. Before free trade in real capital was permitted, economy A used its initial capital stock $O^A K^A$ to produce output equivalent to distance $O^A D$. Economy B used its relatively larger capital stock $O^B K^B$ to produce output equal to $O^B E$.

With real capital mobility, there would be a tendency for equalisation of the real rate of return on capital across both regions. Capital would move internationally until the marginal productivities of capital in the two regions equalise, having fallen in A and risen in B. In final equilibrium, additional capital accumulation in region $A(K^*)$ through imports is matched by decumulation in region B through exports. Combined output rises by GP. Had the autarky equilibrium for each region initially been at Q, the balances in the external accounts would

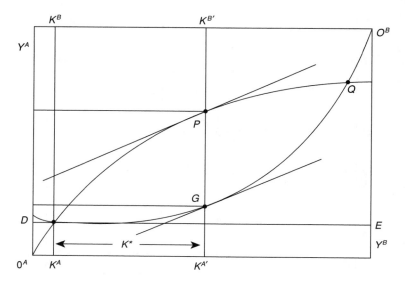

Figure 8.3   The gains from foreign investment (b)

have been reversed after allowing free trade in capital, with region *B* becoming the capital importer instead of *A*.

Though this neoclassical approach to foreign investment neglects the monetary implications of different exchange rate regimes as well as the balance of payments as such, it usefully illustrates the welfare gains from capital transfers. In short, it reveals the benefits of full capital mobility over zero capital mobility where capital mobility is understood in a real sense.

8.3.2   Comparative statics

To further educe the linkages between foreign investment, external balances, national output and national income consider two comparative static exercises under the full real capital mobility assumption. First, an increase in domestic investment opportunities and second an exogenous increase in the supply of foreign capital. Both forms of disturbance can influence an open economy's external accounts and national income.

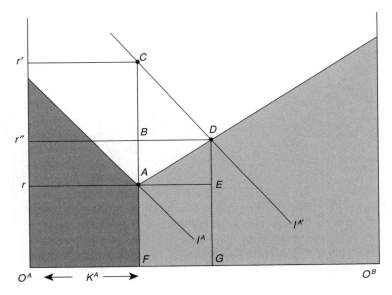

Figure 8.4   An increase in domestic investment

Consider Figure 8.4. In the figure, total wealth equals the combined capital stock throughout and in initial equilibrium with full capital mobility, the return on capital is r. Since competition ensures the return on capital is the value of its marginal product, it follows that the value of A's gross output is the hatched area whereas gross output in B is the dotted area. Following an increase in investment opportunities in A, for instance due to mineral resource discoveries in the home country, domestic demand for capital (I^A) would shift out. If foreign investment was prohibited, the return on country A's capital stock would rise to r'. However, with fully mobile real capital, it only rises to r'' which, when reached, is a Pareto optimum.

In the fully mobile case, greater investment opportunities in A generate capital imports of FG in the transition to the new equilibrium and equivalent capital exports for B. A continues importing real capital willingly exported by B, up to the point where the return on capital in both regions is again equalised.

What of the income effects? Interestingly, the free trade in real capital allows A and B's national income to be higher than otherwise,

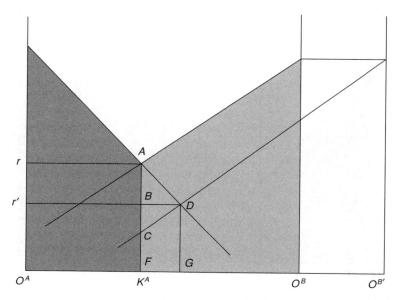

Figure 8.5   An increase in the supply of foreign capital

even though A's national output actually expands while B's contracts. The value of real income transfers eventually recorded as a debit item on A's current account is $FBDG$, the same amount accredited on B's current account. With full capital mobility, A's output is $FCDG$ higher and national income BCD higher than if capital mobility was zero, while B's national output is $FADG$ lower with national income ABD higher. Again, foreign capital helps A produce more domestic output since it augments the capital stock on the aggregate supply side of the economy. The creation of higher income out of a fixed level of wealth necessarily dictates a rise in capital imports matched by rising capital exports abroad. In sum, with changing domestic investment opportunities and fixed wealth in terms of capital goods, the greater is real capital mobility, the higher the income gains may be for both regions.

Consider now the effects on trade in capital of an exogenous increase in B's wealth which enlarges total regional wealth by $O^B O^{B_1}$ as shown in Figure 8.5. Using similar reasoning, it again becomes clear that both A and B share the income gains when free trade in capital is permitted.

The extra wealth enables additional output in *A* (area *ADGF*) and in *B*. *A* gains through the trade by area *ABD* while *B* gains by more than otherwise (area *BCD*). Combined income is *ADC* higher. Such an external disturbance generates a capital trade deficit for *A* and an equivalent capital trade surplus for *B*. Two remaining disturbances could be analysed in this simple comparative static framework; first, a relative rise in *A*'s wealth and second a relative rise in *B*'s demand for capital. From an initial position of balanced trade, either disturbance would generate a trade surplus for *A*, matched by a capital trade deficit for *B* under the assumption of full real capital mobility.

8.4 The adjustment process

The dynamic adjustment process, showing how capital account balances arise as transnational rates of return on capital are equalised, can now be represented by the equation

$$\frac{dK^*}{dt} = \dot{K}^* = KAB = \alpha[(f_{K^*} - \delta) - r^*] \qquad 0 < \alpha < 1 \qquad (8.4)$$

where *KAB* is the real capital account balance and α is an adjustment parameter.

8.4.1 Capital transfer

This arbitrage process is depicted in the simple phase diagram of Figure 8.6. If the net return on foreign capital employed domestically exceeds the world interest rate, then real capital transfer occurs until the equalisation is complete. Up until then, the open economy is a net importer of physical capital, experiencing a real capital account surplus, as indicated by path movement above the horizontal axis. Contrarywise, if real capital is relatively more abundant and the rate of return in the small economy is less than the world rate, the economy is a capital exporter.

This framework also permits transitional dynamic analysis of the effects on the external accounts of exogenous interest rate shocks in major economies. For instance, if there is a fall in the interest rate abroad, then from an initial equilibrium, this would put the economy on a new adjustment path and generate a real international capital account surplus. This surplus would persist until the net marginal

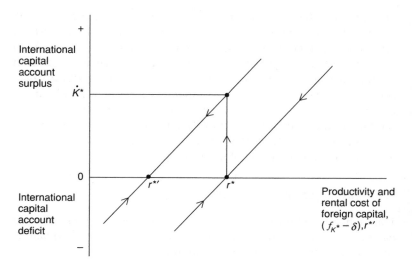

Figure 8.6 Real international capital account adjustment

product of foreign capital in use at home was again equal to the lower external interest rate. On the other hand, if there was a rise in the foreign interest rate the cost of foreign funded capital would increase and real capital would flow out of the open economy, manifesting as a rise in the real capital account deficit.

8.4.2 Tax effects

The domestic fiscal authorities of a small open economy can however affect the size of international capital account imbalances by altering the tax treatment of capital income. For instance, if the tax rate on capital income generated by firms which have benefited from the foreign investment process is t, then the after tax rate of return on capital is $(f_{K^*} - \delta)(1 - t)$. Hence, in the presence of taxes, the equilibrium condition becomes $(f_{K^*} - \delta) = r^*/(1 - t)$. A rise in the tax rate would effectively raise the rental cost of foreign capital from a domestic perspective. This would deter foreign capital inflow as reflected in a temporary international capital account deficit experienced by the small economy, as shown in Figure 8.7.

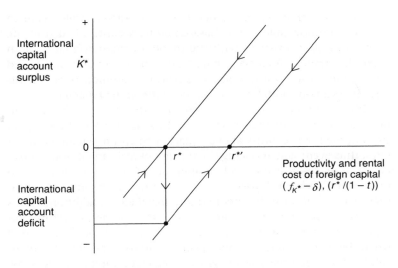

Figure 8.7   Transitional effects of a rise in capital income taxes

Hence, changes in domestic tax policy can exert short run effects on the state of the small economy's external accounts.

8.5.   Interest rates and financial claims

So far, no mention has been made of financial claims to capital, since the analysis of the gains from foreign investment has been strictly in real terms. By introducing financial claims to capital however, it is possible to shed further light on the dynamics of capital transfer across national borders with unrestricted foreign investment.

After Niehans (1984), all capital income may be in the form of dividends paid on equities (q), each one of which represents a claim to a unit of a country's capital stock. The yield is therefore $r = f_k/q$. In initial autarky equilibrium, the market value of the capital stock (q) at home and abroad should be the same as its replacement cost ($\bar{q}$) in accordance with Tobin's q theory of investment.[4]

If the replacement cost of capital goods is the same in the host economy as abroad, but initially $\dfrac{f_k}{q=\bar{q}} > \dfrac{f_{k^*}}{q^*=\bar{q}}$, then the domestic yield on capital must be higher than the foreign yield. Foreign investors are now able to purchase domestic securities issued in the home country. Consistent with the theory of international trade in goods, free trade in financial capital, in the absence of uncertainty and transactions costs, will ultimately establish a common price, in this case the yield on capital, which will clear the unified markets.

With unrestricted foreign investment, the process of trade in financial claims immediately drives up the market value of the capital stock in the home country above replacement cost to equalise interest rates, thus eventually inducing the transfer of real capital from abroad i.e. $r = r^* \Rightarrow q > \bar{q}$ In the final equilibrium, after unrestricted foreign investment has been allowed, $q = \bar{q}$, but this may take some time given that real capital must be imported and installed. As additional units of capital are put into production, the domestic return on capital continues to fall since $f_{kk} < 0$. No further real capital is imported when the market value of capital again equals its original replacement value, at which time the marginal product of capital is the same transnationally.

In the two-region case of Figure 8.8, full capital mobility with financial claims means an initial increase in q above replacement cost in country A, whose capital is relatively more productive, and a fall in q in country B. The corresponding time paths of adjustment of the market values of claims to capital and the capital stock itself are shown in Figure 8.8. Given the initial accumulation and distribution of capital, the opening up at time t_1, of free trade in financial and real capital leads to a jump increase as q rises in A and q falls in B. As long as $q^A/\bar{q}$ is greater than unity in A and $q^B/\bar{q}$ is less than unity in B, capital will be exported by B and imported by A until the market value of capital again reflects its replacement value at time t_2.

8.6   Long-term dynamics

Again, assume a small economy characterised by perfect competition, constant technology, constant returns to scale and full employment. Following Amano (1965), output (Y) is determined by an aggregate Cobb–Douglas production function of the form

$$Y(t) = K(t)^\alpha L(t)^{1-\alpha} \tag{8.5}$$

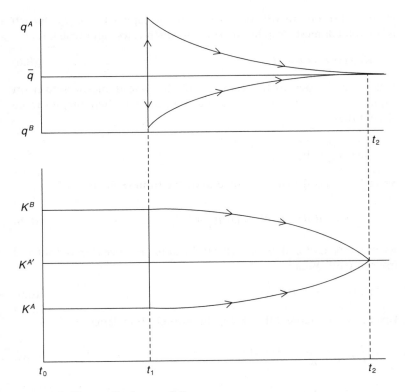

Figure 8.8 Time paths for q and K

where K is the capital stock employed domestically, L is the amount of labour and α is the elasticity of output with respect to capital inputs. Under the above assumptions, α is also capital's share of total output. Therefore the domestic rate of return on capital is $\alpha Y(t) / K(t)$.

Further assuming that domestic saving is a constant fraction, γ, of national income and that labour effort is growing at a constant rate, n, then without capital mobility the output–capital ratio along the equilibrium growth path is n/γ, so that the rate of profit equals $\alpha n/\gamma$.

Assume now that the economy moves from zero capital mobility to full capital mobility at period 0. If the foreign rate of return on capital is

r^*, then the economy will immediately import capital if $r^* < \alpha n / \gamma$. If $K_T(t)$ is the total domestic capital stock, K^* of which is foreign owned, then

$$K_T(t) = K(t) - K^*(t) \tag{8.6}$$

Following a move to full capital mobility, the domestic return on capital equates with the foreign return on capital. Therefore, it can be shown that

$$Y(t) = \frac{r^*}{\alpha} K_T(t) \tag{8.7}$$

Since $L(t) = L(0)E^{nt}$, it is possible to derive from (8.5) and (8.7)

$$K_T(t) = K(0)E^{nt}; K_T(0) = L(0)\left(\frac{\alpha}{r^*}\right)^{\frac{1}{1-\alpha}} \tag{8.8}$$

As we know, national income (Y_n) is the difference between output and interest paid abroad

$$Y_n(t) = Y(t) - r^* K^*(t) \tag{8.9}$$

Lastly, we can express the saving–investment imbalance as

$$\gamma Y(t) + \frac{dK^*(t)}{dt} = \frac{dK_T(t)}{dt} \tag{8.10}$$

Using (8.7) and (8.8) and substituting (8.9) into (8.10) yields

$$
\begin{aligned}
\frac{dK^*(t)}{dt} - r^* \gamma K^*(t) &= \frac{dK_T(t)}{dt} - \gamma Y(t) \\
&= \left(\frac{\frac{dK_T(t)}{dt} - \gamma \frac{Y(t)}{K_T(t)}}{K_T(t)} \right) K_T(0)E^{nt} \\
&= \left(n - \frac{r^* \gamma}{\alpha} \right) K_T(0)E^{nt}
\end{aligned}
\tag{8.11}
$$

Equation (8.11) is a non-homogeneous first-order linear differential equation in $K^*(t)$ whose general solution is given by

$$K^*(t) = C_1 E^{nt} + C_2 E^{r^* \gamma t} \tag{8.12}$$

where

$$C_1 \equiv \frac{n - \frac{r^*\gamma}{\alpha}}{n - r^*\gamma} K_T(0) \quad and$$

$$C_2 \equiv K_T(0) - C_1$$

$C_1 > 0$ since $n > r^*\gamma/\alpha$ and $\alpha < 1$ by assumption. C_2 can be re-expressed as

$$
\begin{aligned}
C_2 &= \frac{(1-\alpha)r^*\gamma}{\alpha(n - r^*\gamma)} K_T(0) - \frac{n - \frac{r^*\gamma}{\alpha}}{(n - r^*\gamma)} K(0) \\
&= \frac{\gamma}{(n - r^*\gamma)} \left(\frac{1-\alpha}{\alpha} r^* K^*(0) - \left(\frac{n}{\gamma} - \frac{r^*}{\alpha} \right) K(0) \right)
\end{aligned}
\tag{8.13}
$$

If $Y_0(0)$ is the value of national income which would have been produced at period 0 without foreign investment, then

$$Y_o(0) = \frac{1}{\alpha} \left(\frac{\alpha n}{\gamma} \right) K(0) < Y(0) = \frac{r^*}{\alpha} (K(0) + K^*(0)) - r^* K^*(0)$$

or

$$\frac{1-\alpha}{\alpha} r^* K^*(0) - \left(\frac{n}{\gamma} - \frac{r^*}{\alpha} \right) K(0) > 0 \tag{8.14}$$

From (8.13) and (8.14), it follows that $C_2 > 0$.

The time path of national income may be derived from (8.7), (8.8), (8.9) and (8.12)

$$Y_n(t) = \frac{(1-\alpha)nr^*}{\alpha(n - r^*\gamma)} K_T(0)E^{nt} - C_2 r^* E^{r^*\gamma t} \tag{8.15}$$

Therefore, we can express the rate of growth of national income, $g(t)$, as

$$g(t) \equiv \frac{dY_n(t)}{dt} \bigg/ Y_n(t) = n + \frac{C_2 r^* E^{r^*\gamma t}}{Y_n(t)} (n - r^*\gamma) \tag{8.16}$$

As $C_2 > 0$, it follows from (8.16) that $g(t) > n$ for $0 \le t < \infty$. However, $g(t)$ declines through time as $C_2 r^* E^{r^*\gamma t}/Y_n(t)$ diminishes. Finally, $g(t) \to n$ as $t \to \infty$.

Therefore, we can conclude that with a move from autarky to full capital mobility, the rate of growth of national income is transitionally higher than the equilibrium growth rate (n) in the very long run.

8.7   Conclusion

This chapter has identified foreign investment, broadly defined, as an additional source of income growth for open trading economies under conditions where physical capital is free to cross country borders. By extending precepts of neoclassical growth theory, it has shown how real capital movements tend to eliminate cross-border differences in rates of return on capital and has also modelled the transitional dynamics of economic growth for a capital importing economy.

The foregoing analysis is in the growth tradition to the extent that it makes the supply side of the open economy the main focus. However, what distinguishes its contribution from the bulk of the literature on economic growth is the explicit identification of foreign capital movements as an important and separate source of output growth for many economies. It suggests that open economies with expanding investment opportunities and high rates of return on capital, such as Australia and the United States, will tend to have current account deficits, whereas countries with relatively low rates of return on capital such as Japan will tend to have corresponding surpluses. Since an open economy with a current account deficit has a rate of capital accumulation in excess of its own rate of saving, it therefore seems misplaced to be concerned about current account imbalances, per se, because such imbalances are only symptomatic of the growth process of internationally integrated economies.

Concerns are also sometimes expressed in external borrower countries that increased capital inflow may not always generate extra tradable production. Notwithstanding some of the difficulties with classifying production as between tradable and non-tradable, a number of points can be made against the proposition that the kind of investment financed matters in any case. First, some non-tradable activities (for example, business services) are probably best thought of as complementary to tradable activities, so that foreign investment in such areas may well ultimately improve the overall competitiveness of tradable industries. Second, foreign funds may directly finance the creation of new tangible assets which would not otherwise be created, as for example with real estate development, and the creation of such assets may simply be motivated by the prospect of a capital gain on the sale of the asset to other foreigners, with no undesirable economic consequences for the host nations.

Indeed, foreign investment in the form of purchases of existing property puts upward pressure on all property values. In this way, foreign investment in property can raise national wealth. Residents who sell existing property assets to non-residents obtain capital gains which would not otherwise have occurred, though of course such capital gains are excluded from conventional measures of residents' national income and may not always be valued efficiently.

In view of the sheer magnitude of real and financial capital movements, it is perhaps surprising that little empirical work has been done to quantify the extent of the macroeconomic income gains to creditor and debtor economies which are attributable to real capital flows.[5] Further empirical research consistent with the above methodology could therefore yield useful results about the process of growth in open economies, and perhaps further strengthen the case against making external imbalances explicit international macroeconomic and commercial policy targets.

9
Financial Globalisation and Emerging Market Crises

The theoretical models expounded in the preceding chapters provide numerous lessons about the macroeconomic effects of financial globalisation. They show that international financial flows accompanying financial globalisation can change current account imbalances, interest rates, exchange rates, national expenditure, output, employment and inflation in host economies.

To the extent that the higher current account deficits and surpluses matching increased capital flows reflect differences between domestic investment over domestic saving, the external balances themselves should not be considered problematic, in and of themselves. External balances reflect increased international trade in saving which can contribute to higher world income growth, consistent with the capital-theoretic approaches outlined earlier.

Host economies benefit because their capital stocks expand through extra investment that enables more production, whereas foreign investors gain to the extent that they can earn higher returns than in their home markets. Moreover, through international portfolio diversification, institutional investors, such as pension, superannuation funds and mutual funds are in principle able to reduce overall volatility of portfolio returns to the extent that movements in national share market prices are unsynchronised.

9.1 Financial crises in emerging markets

Yet, the theory of the gains that can accrue from international capital market integration abstracts from problems that may arise with the channelling of financial flows through the banking and financial sectors of emerging economies. Relatedly, financial globalisation has increased the macroeconomic vulnerability of many of these economies to sharp capital flow reversals of the magnitude witnessed in East Asia and other emerging economies in the late 1990s. In light of the financial distress and economy-wide disruption that financial flow reversals can cause in the short term, it is not surprising that the earlier Keynesian-inspired aversion to highly mobile capital has resurfaced through calls for the reimposition of Bretton Woods-style capital controls for emerging economies.

International investment in financial assets is especially sensitive to changes in investors' expectations, including expected exchange rate devaluations that can spark massive outflows of funds. Indeed, during financial crises, changes in expectations about the exchange rate of any currency can become self-fulfilling as investors rush to sell financial instruments denominated in that currency to minimise capital losses. Under these circumstances, attempts by central banks to mitigate the currency collapse can quickly deplete foreign exchange reserves and push up short-term interest rates.

The adverse consequences of heightened exposure to international investment swings became starkly evident for many East Asian economies during their 1997–98 financial crisis.[1] Although similar financial crises had earlier occurred in Latin America in the 1980s, the sharp reversal in 1997–98 of international capital inflows to previously fast growing Asian economies easily represents the most significant geo-financial adjustment in this relatively new era of globally integrated capital markets (Figure 9.1 & Table 9.1). This reversal of foreign capital, combined with the flight of domestic funds abroad caused massive depreciations against the US dollar of the Indonesian

Table 9.1   Emerging Asian economies: external financing ($US billions)

	1990	1991	1992	1993	1994	1995	1996	1997	1998
Net external financing	26.4	32.6	31.5	39.5	52.4	59.4	63.4	23.5	−6.0
Non debt flows	8.0	9.6	10.9	11.3	11.6	14.3	19.5	18.5	12.7
IMF loans	−1.0	0.2	0.1	0.4	−0.3	−0.4	5.7	...	...
other borrowing	19.3	22.8	20.5	28.1	20.4	45.3	44.3	−0.7	−24.2

Source: IMF (1998: p. 196).

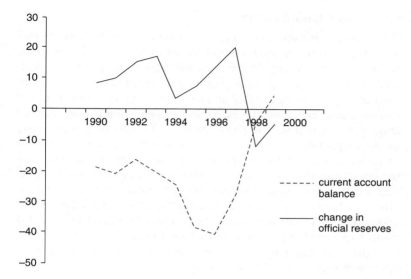

Figure 9.1   Emerging Asian economies: balance of payments ($US billion)

rupiah, Thai baht, Malaysian ringgit, Philippines peso and South Korean won and prompted calls to limit the scale of such flows.

In response, it is argued that tighter restrictions should be put in place by emerging economies to limit the quantum of foreign funds borrowed and lent across their borders. What this interpretation tends to ignore however, is that without earlier capital inflow from abroad, emerging economies would be on a considerably lower plateau of economic development. Average income has increased many fold in emerging economies over recent decades with growth rates significantly above historical averages recorded before the onset of financial globalisation.

The exchange rate management policies of central banks are central to explaining financial crises. For instance, over a lengthy period, East Asian economies either adhered to fixed exchange rates or strictly limited their flexibility, thus providing borrowers and foreign lenders alike with a mistaken degree of exchange rate certainty.

Consequently, a significant part of international borrowings were unhedged against the possibility of large currency depreciations.

9.1.1   Moral hazard and the IMF

When intervening during financial crises in emerging markets, the IMF effectively acts as an international lender of last resort in arranging bridging finance at highly concessional rates to ease external debt-servicing burdens and prevent possible loan default. A criticism of this kind of response from the IMF and its member governments is that it can encourage excessive international borrowing and lending activity and create a 'moral hazard' problem. This is because default risks may be underestimated if the IMF is automatically assumed to provide financial assistance when crises occur. It can be argued that IMF bail-out assistance effectively subsidises those foreign lenders with longer-term loans who are unable to liquidate their assets quickly and would otherwise have lost funds through default action. Against these views and in defence of IMF actions however, it may be argued that the IMF needs to respond as it does in order to minimise financial distress in emerging economies that arises because their banking and financial systems of those economies are so fragile.

9.1.2   Financial sector problems

For instance, prudential supervision of domestic banks, the institutions that channel the bulk of foreign lending in emerging markets, has been weak and non-systematic.[2] Banks in particular were established with minimal capitalisation and a lack of effective competition that allowed local banks to charge high interest rates to domestic borrowers, in turn encouraging further foreign borrowing.

Information on the extent of non-performing loans in emerging economies and on the nature of the linkages between governments and business can also be limited. This lack of transparency obscures the nature of the underlying structural problems of financial institutions. The reversal of capital inflow to East Asia and other emerging markets happened, for instance, after foreign investors sold off East Asian financial assets on a large scale on realising that their funds were at greater risk than previously thought. In the most severely affected economies, the prices of bonds, equities and currencies plummeted, damaging their financial systems with consequences for real economic activity[3] (Tables 9.2 and 9.3).

The impact of the financial crisis on the real sectors of select Asian economies worst affected is evident from Figure 9.2 which shows the extent of the recessions which followed.

Table 9.2 Stock market indices, per cent change July–November 1997

Indonesia	–37
Korea	–34
Malaysia	–56
Philippines	–45
Thailand	–52

Table 9.3 Exchange rate movements, per cent change June 1997–March 1998

	Against $US	Against yen	Nominal effective	Real effective
Korea	–39.0	–31.0	–35.3	–30.3
Indonesia	–73.9	–70.6	–71.4	–63.2
Malaysia	–32.3	–23.5	–24.8	–23.6
Philippines	–31.0	–22.1	–24.8	–21.8
Thailand	–37.5	–29.4	–31.8	–27.1

Source: International Monetary Fund, IFS.

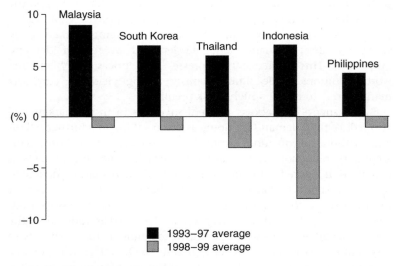

Figure 9.2 Percentage change in GDP
Source: IMF (1998) *World Economic Outlook*, May, Consensus Forecasts.

Yet, the substantial financial asset divestment by foreign investors, including the large US-based hedge funds was not the only factor that generated the subsequent East Asian crisis. In addition, the panic withdrawal by resident investors of their own funds from local financial institutions converted a sharp correction of financial asset prices into the major financial crisis that followed.

9.2   International portfolio adjustment and asset prices

Having identified reasons why capital can suddenly exit emerging economies, it remains to explain the process of international portfolio switches and how international capital flow reversals cause asset prices and national wealth positions to contract with reference to Figure 9.3.

In the left panel of the figure, the total pre-crisis demand for emerging market assets is comprised of demand by local investors themselves (R_d^A) and demand by foreigners (F_d^*). The supply of emerging market assets is shown by the A_S^A schedule and the pre-crisis equilibrium price of assets in emerging markets is P_0^A. The right side panel of the figure conveys the inverse relationship between asset prices in emerging markets on the vertical axis and their yields on the horizontal axis, with pre-crisis equilibrium yields shown at i_0^A. A sudden portfolio switch by foreign investors out of emerging markets firstly shifts the asset demand schedule leftward as foreign demand evaporates. This immediately depresses asset prices to P_1^A and net worth positions while simultaneously raising yields in emerging markets to i_1^A to reflect a higher risk premium.

But, as mentioned above, resident investors in those markets will also reduce their demand for home assets, resulting in a further sell off and withdrawal of funds from local financial institutions. This secondary reduction in demand for assets in emerging markets is conveyed in Figure 9.3 by the further shift of the demand schedule to $R_d^{A'}$ with the result that asset prices fall further to P_2^A. This withdrawal of funds, first by foreign investors then by domestic investors from emerging market institutions may well be described as 'rational' to the extent that all investors were attempting to eliminate their exposure to a systemic collapse ahead of other investors. Of course, it is possible that domestic investors could act first and prompt foreigners to follow suit. Either way, local asset prices ultimately collapse.

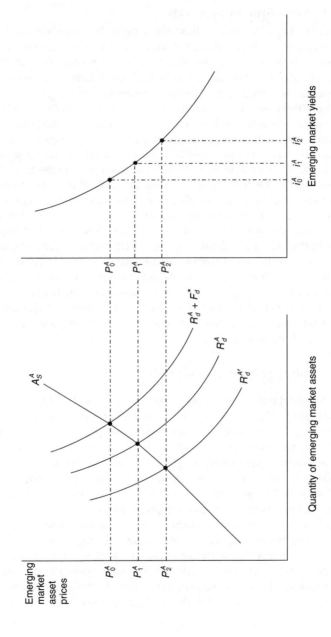

Figure 9.3 Effects of portfolio switch on emerging market asset prices and yields

9.2.1   Rest-of-the-world effects

When foreign investors adjust their portfolios by switching out of emerging markets to safer alternatives, the foreign capital that quits these markets is reinvested elsewhere in the world. This then keeps interest rates low and asset values high elsewhere and sustains extra economic activity and trade opportunities in those regions.

The effects on the rest of the world of the portfolio switch-out of emerging markets to alternative assets can be modelled as the counterpart to the earlier analysis contained in Figure 9.3. This is shown in Figure 9.4 by a rise in demand for financial instruments in the rest of the world (ROW) which raises ROW asset prices from P_0^* to P_1^* and lowers yields from i_0^* to i_1^*. To the extent that resident investors in emerging markets switch funds to foreign assets out of their own assets, there is a further increase in demand for ROW assets which pushes ROW asset prices up to P_2^* and lowers ROW yields to i_2^*. If it happened that in the pre-crisis equilibrium, asset yields in emerging markets and in the rest of the world had been equal (that is, $i_0^* = i_0^A$), then the post-crisis yield differential would reflect the size of the post-crisis risk premium in emerging markets. This is shown on the horizontal axis of the right panel of Figure 9.4 as the distance between the post-crisis yield on emerging market instruments, i_2^A, and the post-crisis yield in the rest of the world, i_2^*.

9.3   Policy responses: an analogy [4]

The financial turbulence in emerging economies in the wake of the crises of the late 1990s has revived demands for restrictions on the volume of international capital flows. This international public policy prescription is, however, essentially at odds with the economic proposition that foreign saving contributes positively to economic development. In what follows, an analogy is therefore developed to suggest why restoring capital or exchange controls is an ill-advised means of improving long-term economic welfare in emerging economies.

According to the standard theory of economic growth, saving acts like a vehicle carrying an economy from one stage of development to another. However, though not explicitly recognised in the traditional neoclassical model of economic growth, but as shown in the analysis of the previous chapter, saving can come from both domestic and foreign sources. To get to the destination of higher national income, domestic

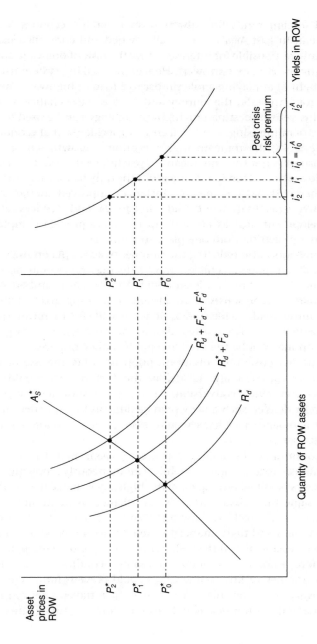

Figure 9.4 Effects of portfolio switch on asset prices and yields in the rest of the world

and foreign funds flow through an emerging economy's financial system. In East Asia's case, locally-owned and controlled banks were mainly responsible for intermediating the flow of domestic and foreign saving to ultimate borrowers. Hence, the banking system itself can be thought of as playing a role similar to a road or highway. The sounder the road, the safer the journey and the lower the chance of accidents.

This vehicle–destination–highway analogy can be used to compare ways of minimising occasional crises, or accidents, that economies may have along the route to higher economic growth. Of course, road transport is not the only means of reaching a desired destination, just as domestic and foreign saving is not the only factor that contributes to higher national income. For instance, improved human capital or greater liberalisation of trade in goods and services also assist development, just as air and rail transport provide complementary modes of getting from one place to another.

One option for reducing the number of accidents on highways is to prohibit imported vehicles, thus reducing the overall flow of road traffic. This option has been adopted by Malaysia and advocated by numerous economists. But, although limiting road traffic would minimise road accident risk, it is also likely, to mean that fewer passengers can reach their desired destination, implying that the option may not be the preferred public policy response.

Another crisis minimisation option is to tax the use of imported vehicles differentially. Relatedly, the 'Tobin tax', would apply to foreign currency conversions arising from short-term capital flows worldwide. Yet, such a tax would be difficult to implement in practice and avoidance problems would arise if some economies refused to participate.

Continuing the analogy, it would seem that the best way to minimise road accidents, while simultaneously allowing as much travel as possible, is to upgrade the highway to make travel safer and at the same time ensure there is surveillance of traffic flows to detect instances of reckless driving. With reference to the emerging economies and their financial systems, crisis prevention would therefore be best achieved through major reform of banking practices.

More information about economic conditions and improved transparency of financial dealings could prevent future crises, just as advisory signs on highways make road travel safer. Arms-length prudential authorities could also perform a surveillance role by policing the capital adequacy ratios of banks to ensure financial speed limits are not exceeded. Such fundamental reforms of financial practices need to be in place and recognised as such by foreign investors, including international banks to attract sustainable capital inflows.

In short, the recent financial crises in East Asia and other emerging economies have exposed major structural weaknesses in their domestic banking and financial systems, which have acted as the major conduits of foreign saving. More specifically, these crises have underscored the need for a more robust system of bank supervision in line with international standards, for example as set out in the principles of prudent banking recommended by the Bank for International Settlements. With a sounder financial infrastructure, appropriately monitored to prevent reckless lending, foreign saving can continue to contribute positively to economic growth in emerging economies. Greater international capital integration is unlikely to accelerate until such financial reforms are firmly established and recognised by international investors, including major multinational banks.

9.4   The future of financial globalisation

The general finding of international trade theory that free trade in goods enhances economic welfare has strong support from international economists and international institutions such as the WTO whose very brief is to progress trade liberalisation. Large trading blocs, such as the North American Free Trade Agreement (NAFTA), the European Union and the Asia-Pacific Economic Cooperation forum (APEC) have been established for the very purpose of encouraging greater cross-border trade in goods and services by dismantling impediments to trade, such as import tariffs.

Although the WTO has also been pursuing international agreement on expanding trade in financial services, the idea that international trade in saving similarly confers mutual welfare gains on contracting parties is not as widely recognised. Yet, allowing international capital to continue flowing freely can improve economic welfare in emerging economies for it releases those economies from the constraint of their own saving levels. In this way, foreign savings can complement domestic savings and play an important role in the process of economic growth, for it permits domestic capital accumulation to be higher than otherwise. Meanwhile, the national income of creditor countries may rise to the extent that international lenders earn higher returns than otherwise.

The main objection to the argument about the benefits of liberalising the flow of funds across borders is that reversals of capital inflows make economies more susceptible to crises. In other words, the heightened international interdependence of financial markets exposes economies to the risk of international capital flight. Capital flight in response to new information about exchange rate risk, default risk or deteriorating fiscal and monetary policy settings can impose substantial short-term costs on emerging economies through higher interest rates and lost output, as well as through large exchange rate depreciations and the associated higher inflation. Nonetheless, it should be recognised that any sharp redirection of international investment funds from emerging economies provides a strong signal to domestic policy-makers that further growth-enhancing reform is necessary.

Reversing the tide of financial globalisation is likely to be more difficult in practice than ever before, although international financial crises may stall it temporarily. The key difference between the international economic and political environment of today and that of the last globalisation era that ended with the First World War is that there now exists a well-established supranational institutional framework fostering international economic exchanges. In contrast, in the first globalisation era all economic institutions were nationally based and independent international institutions encouraging international exchange did not exist.

In contrast, the present framework is comprised of numerous supranational economic institutions, such as the Bank for International Settlements, the World Trade Organisation, the International Monetary Fund, the World Bank and other United Nations affiliated bodies. Generally speaking, these institutions advocate compatible, pro-globalisation objectives. Indeed, a major rationale for these organisations, most of which under one guise or another have been operating for over half a century, is to encourage and facilitate increased global exchange.

At the start of a new millennium, the so-called 'Washington consensus' on the net economic benefits of free international trade and investment remains intact. International organisations continue to promote freer international trade, investment and capital market, though not always with success. For example, the attempt by the OECD to systemise the treatment of foreign investment worldwide through the Multilateral Investment Agreement faltered in part due to strong opposition from economic nationalist groups in many countries.

Yet, further scope remains for integrating international goods, services and asset markets. For instance, trade to GDP ratios are still relatively small for many economies in the world, including large economies like the United States and Japan. Moreover, most of the investment that occurs in national economies is still funded by domestically generated saving, suggesting considerable potential remains for exploiting the gains from global finance.

Notes

1 Evolution of the international financial system

1. Edelstein (1982) elaborates.
2. See International Monetary Fund (1997, p. 242).
3. Eichengreen (1996) and McKinnon (1993) discuss the history of the international monetary system at length.
4. See also United Nations (1949).
5. Burtless *et al.* (1998) address common fallacies about globalisation.

2 Accounting and measurement issues

1. In practice, exchange rate movements and gold price fluctuations also affect the domestic currency value of official reserves.
2. It is assumed that private households save and private and public enterprises invest, although in practice household expenditure on private dwellings is a significant component of private investment and retained earnings and undistributed income of enterprises comprise part of measured saving.
3. See Tobin (1969).
4. Consumer durables are included on the basis that they yield a stream of benefits through time, even though they comprise a relatively small share of total assets.
5. See Makin and Robson (1999) for a comparison of trade and capital weighted index measures of the Australian dollar.

3 Early balance of payments models

1. See Goldstein and Khan (1985).
2. See also Corden (1982, 1994), Dornbusch (1980) and Prachowny (1984).
3. See also Frenkel and Mussa (1995).
4. See Branson (1977) and Allen and Kenen (1978), amongst others.
5. See Kouri (1976), and Dornbusch and Fischer (1980).

4 Intertemporal trade, capital mobility and interest rates

1. Amongst others, Webb (1970), Sachs (1982), Frenkel and Razin (1987), Makin (1994a), and Obstfeld and Rogoff (1996) have expounded variants of the Fisherian intertemporal open economy model.
2. Keynes (1936, chapter 13) contains the classic pessimistic view of financial market activity.
3. As proposed by Dornbusch and Giovannini (1990).

4. As suggested by Frankel (1989).
5. See Marston (1995) on empirical evidence.

5   Financial flows, interest rates and exchange rates

1. Aliber (1973), Isard (1995) and Taylor (1995) outline arbitrage-based interpretations of uncovered interest rate parity.
2. Dornbusch (1992) and Rogoff (1996) survey the theory and evidence for purchasing power parity.
3. See also Ghosh and Ostry (1995).

6   Macroeconomic policy in the open economy

1. Alternative advanced expositions of MF genus models are included in Dornbusch (1980), Frenkel and Razin (1985), Marston (1985), Frenkel and Mussa (1985) and Scarth (1988).
2. Dernburg (1989) uses a similar mathematical approach.
3. See Duesenberry (1949), Friedman (1957) and Modigliani (1970).
4. See Jorgenson (1974), Tobin (1969) and Abel (1990).
5. See Argy and Salop (1979) and Branson and Buiter (1983).
6. See Barro (1974,1989), Buchanan (1976) and Seater (1993).

8   Foreign capital and economic growth

1. See McDougall (1960), Amano (1965), Kemp (1966), Bardhan (1967), Ruffin (1979), Grubel (1980), Niehans (1984) and Pitchford (1995).
2. Conventional trade theory concludes that under certain conditions, including constant returns to scale, factor price equalisation can occur from trade in goods alone, without any trade in factors. Hence, cross-border equality of marginal products can exist before allowing capital movements.
3. If we allow for depreciation of the capital stock, the equilibrium return to capital becomes $f_k - d_e$ where d_e is the deprecation rate. This follows because $Y_n = f(K, L) - d_e K$ and with constant returns to scale $Y_n = (f_n(K, L) - d_e)K + f_L(K, L)L$.
4. See Tobin (1969) and Hayashi (1982).
5. Exceptions with reference to the Australian experience are Layton and Makin (1993).

9   Financial globalisation and emerging market crises

1. On the East Asian crisis, see also Goldstein (1998) and Makin (1999a).
2. Stiglitz (1985) analyses bank lending to risky borrowers when information is imperfect.
3. Kindleberger (1996) provides an historical account of banking and financial crises.
4. This section draws on Makin (1999b).

Bibliography

Abel, A.B. (1990) 'Consumption and Investment', in B.M. Friedman and F.H. Hahn (eds), *Handbook of Monetary Economics*, vol. 2, North-Holland, Amsterdam, ch. 14, pp. 726–78.

Agarwal, J.P. (1980) 'Determinants of Foreign Direct Investment: A Survey', *Weltwirtschaftliches Archiv*, vol. 116(4), pp. 739–73.

Alexander, S.S. (1952) 'Effects of a Devaluation on a Trade Balance', *International Monetary Fund Staff Papers* vol. 1(2), pp. 263–78; reprinted in R.E. Caves and H. G. Johnson (eds), (1968) *A.E.A. Readings in International Economics*, vol. 11, Richard Irwin, Homewood, Illinois, pp. 359–73.

Alexander, S.S. (1959) 'Effects of a Devaluation: A Simplified Synthesis of Elasticities and Absorption Approaches', *American Economic Review*, vol. 49(1), pp. 22–42.

Aliber, R.Z. (1973) 'The Interest Rate Parity Theorem: A Reinterpretation', *Journal of Political Economy*, vol. 81(6), pp. 1451–59.

Allen, P.R. and Kenen, P.B. (1978) *Asset Markets, Exchange Rates, and Economic Integration: A Synthesis*, Cambridge University Press, Cambridge.

Amano, A. (1965) 'International Capital Movements and Economic Growth', *Kyklos*, vol. 18(1), pp. 693–99.

Argy, V. (1994) *International Macroeconomics*, Routledge, London.

Argy, V. and Salop, J. (1979) 'Price and Output Effects of Monetary and Fiscal Policy Under Flexible Exchange Rates', *IMF Staff Papers*, vol. 26(2), pp. 224–56.

Artus, J. and Rhomberg, R. (1973) 'A Multilateral Exchange Rate Model', *IMF Staff Papers*, vol. 20, pp. 591–611.

Bailey, M. (1957) 'Saving and the Rate of Interest', *Journal of Political Economy*, vol. 65(4), pp. 279–305.

Balassa, B. (1964) 'The Purchasing Power Parity Doctrine: A Re-appraisal', *Journal of Political Economy*, vol. 72(6), pp. 584–96.

Bardhan, P.K. (1967) 'Optimum Foreign Borrowing', in K. Shell (ed.) *Essays on the Theory of Optimal Economic Growth*, MIT Press, Cambridge, Massachusetts, pp. 117–28.

Barro, R. and Sala-I-Martin, X. (1995) *Economic Growth*, McGraw Hill, New York.

Barro, R.J. (1974) 'Are Government Bonds Net Wealth?', *Journal of Political Economy*, vol. 82(5), pp. 1095–117.

Barro, R.J. (1989) 'The Ricardian Approach to Budget Deficits', *Journal of Economic Perspectives*, vol. 3, pp. 37–54.

Bayoumi, T. (1990) 'Saving-Investment Correlations: Immobile Capital Government Policy or Endogenous Behaviour?', *IMF Staff Papers*, vol. 37(3), pp. 361–87.

Bhagwhati, J. (1998) 'The Capital Myth: The Difference Between Trade in Widgets and Dollars', *Foreign Affairs*, vol. 77(3), May/June.

Bickerdike, C.F. (1920) 'The Instability of Foreign Exchange', *Economic Journal*, vol. 30, March, pp. 118–22.

Black, S.W. (1976) 'Multilateral and Bilateral Measures of Effective Exchange Rates in a World Model of Traded Goods', *Journal of Political Economy*, vol. 84(3), pp. 615–21.

Branson, W. and Henderson, D. (1985) 'The Specification and Influence of Asset Markets', in R. Jones and P. Kenen (eds), *Handbook of International Economics*, vol. 2, North Holland, Amsterdam.

Branson, W.H. (1977) 'Asset Markets and Relative Prices in Exchange Rate Determination', *Sozialwissenschaftliche Annalen des Instituts fur hohere Studien*, vol. 1, pp. 69–89; reprinted as *Reprint in International Finance*, No. 20, International Finance Section, Princeton University, New Jersey.

Branson, W.H. and Buiter, W.H. (1983) 'Monetary and Fiscal Policy and Flexible Exchange Rates', in J.S. Bhandari and B.H. Putnam (eds), *Economic Interdependence and Flexible Exchange Rates*, MIT Press, Cambridge, Massachusetts, ch. 9, pp. 251–85.

Bruce, N. and Purvis, D. (1985) 'The Specification of Goods and Factor Markets in Open Economy Macroeconomic Models', in R. Jones and P. Kenen (eds), *Handbook of International Economics*, vol. 2, North Holland, Amsterdam.

Bryant, R. (1987) *International Financial Intermediation*, Brookings, Washington.

Buchanan, J.M. (1976) 'Barro on the Ricardian Equivalence Theorem', *Journal of Political Economy*, vol. 84(2), pp. 337–42.

Buiter, W.H. (1981) 'Time Preference and International Lending in an Overlapping Generations Model', *Journal of Political Economy*, vol. 89(4), pp. 769–97.

Buiter, W.H. and Purvis, D.D. (1983) 'Oil, Disinflation and Export Competitiveness: A Model of the 'Dutch Disease'', in J. Bhandari and B.H. Putman (eds) *Economic Interdependence and Flexible Exchange Rates*, MIT Press, Cambridge, Massachusetts, ch. 8, pp. 221–47.

Burtless, G., Lawrence, R., Litan, R., and Shapiro, R. (eds), (1998) *Globaphobia: Confronting Fears About Open Trade*, Brookings Institution, Washington DC.

Canzoneri, M. and Henderson, D. (1991) *Monetary Policy in Interdependent Economies*, MIT Press, Massachusetts.

Caves, R. (1971) 'International Corporations: The Industrial Economics of Foreign Investment', *Economica*, vol. 38, February, pp. 1–27.

Claassen, E. (1996) *Global Monetary Economics*, Oxford University Press, Oxford.

Cohen, D. (1998) *The Wealth of the World and the Poverty of Nations*, MIT Press, Massachusetts.

Connolly, M. (1978) 'The Monetary Approach to an Open Economy: The Fundamental Theory', in B.H. Putnam and D.S. Wilford (eds), *The Monetary Approach to International Adjustment*, Praeger, New York, ch. 1, pp. 6–18.

Contractor, F. (1998) *Economic Transformation in Emerging Economies: The Role of Investment, Trade and Finance*, Elsevier, New York.

Corden, M. (1994) *Economic Policy, Exchange Rates and the International System*, Oxford University Press, Oxford.

Corden, W.M. (1982) 'Exchange Rate Protection', in R.N. Cooper et.al., *The International Monetary System Under Flexible Exchange Rates*, Ballinger, Cambridge, Massachusetts.

Corden, W.M. and Neary, J.P. (1982) 'Booming Sector and De-Industrialisation in a Small Open Economy', *Economic Journal*, vol. 92, pp. 825–48.

Corden, W.M. (1997) 'How Would a Fiscal Expansion Affect the Exchange Rate?', in M. Blejer and T. Ter-Minassian (eds), *Macroeconomic Dimensions of Public Finance*, Routledge, London.

Cumby, R.E. (1988) 'Is it Risk? Explaining Deviations from Uncovered Interest Parity', *Journal of Monetary Economics*, vol. 22, pp. 279–99.

Cumby, R.E. and Mishkin, F.S. (1986) 'The International Linkage of Real Interest Rates: The European-US Connection', *Journal of International Money and Finance*, vol. 5, pp. 5–23.

De Grauwe (1996) *International Money*, 2nd ed., Oxford University Press, Oxford.

De Grauwe, P. (1992) *The Economics of Monetary Integration*, Oxford University Press, Oxford.

Dernburg, T.F. (1989) *Global Macroeconomics*, Harper and Row, New York.

Diewert, W.E. (1976) 'Exact and Superlative Index Numbers', *Journal of Econometrics*, vol. 4, pp. 115–45.

Diewert, W.E. (1989) 'Index Numbers', in J. Eatwell et. al. (eds), *The New Palgrave Dictionary of Economics and Finance*, London: Macmillan.

Dooley, M.P., Frankel, J.A. and Mathieson J. (1987) 'International Capital Mobility: What Do Saving-Investment Correlations Tell Us?', *IMF Staff Papers*, vol. 34(3), pp. 503–30.

Dornbusch, R. (1973) 'Devaluation, Money and Non-Traded Goods', *American Economic Review*, vol. 63(5), pp. 871–83.

Dornbusch, R. (1976) 'Expectations and Exchange Rate Dynamics', *Journal of Political Economy*, vol. 84(6), pp. 1161–76.

Dornbusch, R. (1980) *Open Economy Macroeconomics*, Basic Books, New York.

Dornbusch, R. (1992) 'Purchasing Power Parity', in J. Eatwell, M. Milgate and P. Newman (eds), *The New Palgrave Dictionary of Economics*, London: Macmillan.

Dornbusch, R. and Fischer, S. (1980) 'Exchange Rates and the Current Account', *American Economic Review*, vol. 70(5), pp. 960–71.

Dornbusch, R. and Giovannini, A. (1990) 'Monetary Policy in an Open Economy', in B.M. Friedman and F.H. Hahn (eds), *Handbook of Monetary Economics*, vol. 2, North-Holland, Amsterdam, ch. 23, pp. 1231–303.

Dumas, B. (1995) 'Partial Equilibrium vs General-Equilibrium Models of International Capital Market Equilibrium', in R. van der Ploeg (ed.) *Handbook of International Macroeconomics*, London: Blackwell.

Dutton, M.M. (1993) 'Real Interest Rate Parity: New Measures and Tests', *Journal of International Money and Finance*, vol. 12, pp. 62–77.

Edelstein, M. (1982) *Overseas Investment in the Age of High Imperialism: The United Kingdom 1850–1914*, Columbia University Press, New York.

Eichengreen, B. (1996) *Globalising Capital: History of the International Monetary System*, Princeton University Press, Princeton.

Eisner, R. (1988) 'Extended Accounts for National Income and Product', *Journal of Economic Literature*, vol. 26, pp. 1611–84.

Fama, E.F. and Miller, M.H. (1972) *The Theory of Finance*, Holt, Rinehart and Winston, New York.

Feldstein, M. (1983) 'Domestic Saving and International Capital Movements in the Long Run and the Short Run', *European Economic Review*, vol. 21, pp. 129–51.

Feldstein, M. and Horioka, C. (1980) 'Domestic Saving and International Capital Flows', *Economic Journal*, vol. 90, June, pp. 314–29.

Fisher, I. (1930) *The Theory of Interest*, New York: Macmillan.

Fishlow, A. (1988) 'External Borrowing and Debt Management', in R. Dornbusch and F. Helmers (eds), *The Open Economy: Tools for Policymakers in Developing Countries*, Oxford University Press, London, ch. 6, pp. 187–222.

Fleming, J. (1962) 'Domestic Financial Policies Under Fixed and Under Floating Exchange Rates', *IMF Staff Papers*, vol. 9(4), pp. 369–79.

Frankel, J.A. (1989) 'Quantifying International Capital Mobility in the 1980s', *NBER Working Paper, No. 2856*, National Bureau of Economic Research.

Frenkel, J.A. and Mussa, M.L. (1985) 'Asset Markets, Exchange Rates and the Balance of Payments', in R.W. Jones and P.B. Kenen (eds), *Handbook of International Economics*, vol. 2, North-Holland, Amsterdam, ch. 14, pp. 679–747.

Frenkel, J. and Razin, A. (1992) *Fiscal Policies and the World Economy*, 2nd ed., MIT Press, Massachusetts.

Friedman, M. (1957) *A Theory of the Consumption Function*, Princeton University Press, New Jersey.

Froot, K. and Rogoff, K. (1995) 'Perspectives on PPP and Long-Run Real Exchange Rates', in G. Grossman and K. Rogoff (eds), *Handbook of International Economics*, vol. 3, North Holland, Amsterdam.

Fukao, M. and Hanazaki, M. (1987) 'The Internationalisation of Financial Markets', *OECD Economic Studies*, vol. 8, pp. 35–92.

Gaab, W., Franziol, M. and Horner, M. (1986) 'On Some International Parity Conditions: An Empirical Investigation', *European Economic Review*, vol. 30(3), pp. 683–713.

Gartner, M. (1993) *Macroeconomics under Flexible Exchange Rates*, Harvester Wheatsheaf.

Ghosh, A. and Ostry, J. (1995) 'The Current Account in Developing Countries: A Perspective from the Consumption-Smoothing Approach', *World Bank Economic Review*, vol. 9(2), pp. 305–33.

Goldstein, M. and Khan, M.S. (1985) 'Income and Price Effects in Foreign Trade', in R.W. Jones and P.B. Kenen (eds), *Handbook of International Economics*, North-Holland, Amsterdam, ch. 20, pp. 1041–105.

Goldstein, M. (1998) *The Asian Crisis: Causes, Cures and Systemic Implications*, Institute for International Economics, No. 55, Washington, DC.

Goldstein, M. and Mussa, M. (1993) 'The Integration of World Capital Markets', IMF Working Paper, 93/95, International Monetary Fund, December.

Grossman, G. and Helpman, E. (1991) *Innovation and Growth in the Global Economy*, Massachusetts: MIT Press.

Grubel, H. G. (1968) 'Internationally Diversified Portfolios: Welfare Gains and Capital Flows', *American Economic Review*, vol. 58(5), pp. 1299–314.

Grubel, H.G. (1987) 'Foreign Investment', in J. Eatwell, M. Milgate and P. Newman (eds), *The New Palgrave Dictionary of Economics*, vol. 2, Macmillan, London, pp.403–6.

Hayashi, F. (1982) 'Tobin's Marginal q and Average q: a Neo-Classical Interpretation', *Econometrica*, vol. 50(1), pp. 213–24.

Hicks, J. (1946) *Value and Capital*, Clarendon Press, Oxford.

Hinshaw, R. (1975) 'Non-Traded Goods and the Balance of Payments', *Journal of Economic Literature*, vol. 13(2), pp. 475–9.

Hume, D. (1752) 'Of the Balance of Trade', in R.N. Cooper (ed.) (1989) *International Finance – Selected Readings*, Penguin, Harmondsworth, pp. 25–37.

Inada, K. (1963) 'On a Two-Sector Model of Economic Growth: Comments and a Generalization', *Review of Economic Studies*, vol. 30 June, pp. 119–27.

International Monetary Fund (1977) *The Monetary Approach to the Balance of Payments*, IMF, Washington, D.C.

International Monetary Fund (1999) *International Capital Markets: Developments, Prospects and Key Policy Issues*, International Monetary Fund, November, Washington, DC.

International Monetary Fund *World Economic Outlook*, International Monetary Fund, Washington, DC, various issues.

Irwin, D. (1995) 'The GATT in Historical Perspective', *American Economic Review*, vol. 85, May, pp. 323–8.

Isard, P. (1992) 'Uncovered Interest Parity', in J. Eatwell, M. Milgate and P. Newman (eds), *The Palgrave Dictionary of Money and Finance*, London: Macmillan.

Isard, P. (1995) *Exchange Rate Economics*, Cambridge University Press, New York.

Johnson, H. (1977) 'The Monetary Approach to the Balance of Payments: A Nontechnical Guide', *Journal of International Economics*, vol. 7, pp. 251–68.

Jorgenson, D.W. (1971) 'Economic Studies of Investment Behaviour: A Survey', *Journal of Economic Literature*, vol. 9, pp. 1111–47.

Kemp, M. (1966) 'The Gain from International Trade and Investment: A Neo-Heckscher-Ohlin Approach', *American Economic Review*, vol. 56(3), September, pp. 788–809.

Kenen, P.B. (1985) 'Macroeconomic Theory and Policy: How the Closed Economy Was Opened', in R.W. Jones and P.B. Kenen (eds) *Handbook of International Economics*, vol. 2, ch. 13, pp. 625–77.

Kenen, P. (1995) *Understanding Interdependence: The Macroeconomics of the Open Economy*, Princeton University Press, New Jersey.

Keynes, J.M. (1936) *The General Theory of Employment, Interest and Money*, Macmillan, London.

Keynes, J.M. (1941) 'The Origins of the Clearing Union, 1940–1942', in *The Collected Writings of J.M. Keynes*, Macmillan for the Royal Economic Society, London, vol. XXV, pp. 1–144.

Kindleberger, C.P. (1987) *International Capital Movements*, Cambridge, Cambridge University Press.

Kindleberger, C.P. (1996) *Manias, Panics and Crashes: A History of Financial Crises*, 3rd ed, Wiley, New York.

Kouri, P. (1976) 'The Exchange Rate and the Balance of Payments in the Short Run and in the Long Run: A Monetary Approach', *Scandinavian Journal of Economics*, vol. 78(2), pp. 280–304.

Kreinin, M. and Officer, L. (1978) 'The Monetary Approach to the Balance of Payments: A Survey', *Princeton Studies in International Finance*, No. 43, International Finance Section, Princeton University.

Krueger, A. (1983) *Exchange Rate Determination*, Cambridge University Press, New York.

Krugman, P. (1979) 'A Model of Balance of Payments Crises', *Journal of Money, Credit and Banking*, vol. 11, pp. 311–25.

Krugman, P. (1991) *Has the Adjustment Process Worked?*, Institute for International Economics, Washington DC.

Layton, A.P. and Makin, A. (1993) 'Estimates of the Macroeconomic Impact of Foreign Investment', *International Economic Journal*, vol. 7(4), pp. 35–42.

Leiderman, L. and Blejer, M.I. (1988) 'Modelling and Testing Ricardian Equivalence: A Survey', *IMF Staff Papers*, vol. 35(1), pp. 1–35.

Lewis, K.K. (1995) 'International Financial Markets', in G. Grossman and K. Rogoff (eds), *Handbook of International Economics*, Amsterdam: North-Holland.

MacDougall, G.D.A. (1960) 'The Benefits and Costs of Private Investment from Abroad: A Theoretical Approach', *Economic Record*, Special Issue (March). Reprinted in R.E. Caves and H.G. Johnson (eds), (1968) *A.E.A. Readings in International Economics*, vol. 11, Richard Irwin, Homewood, Illinois, ch. 10, pp. 172–203.

Machlup, F. (1939) 'The Theory of Foreign Exchanges: Part I', *Economica*, vol. 6, pp. 375–98.

Maciejewski, E.B. (1983) "Real' Effective Exchange Rate Indices', IMF Staff Papers, September, pp. 491–541.

Makin, A. (1989) 'Is the Current Account Deficit Sustainable?', *Australian Economic Review*, 2nd Quarter, pp. 29–33.

Makin, A. (1993) 'Capital Market Integration and National Wealth', *Australian Economic Review*, 2nd quarter, pp. 61–70.

Makin, A. (1994a) *International Capital Mobility and External Account Determination*, Macmillan and St Martins Press, London and New York.

Makin, A. (1994b) 'Open Economy Measures of Wealth and Hicksian Income' *Open Economies Review*, vol. 5(4), pp. 361–9.

Makin, A. (1995) 'Inflation Distortion of the External Accounts', *Journal of Economic Studies*, vol. 22(1), pp. 58–65.

Makin, A. (1996) *Open Economy Macroeconomics*, Addison Wesley Longman, Melbourne.

Makin, A. (1998a) 'A Dependent Economy Model of Public Expenditure and the Exchange Rate', *International Review of Economics and Finance*, vol. 7(4), pp. 453–63.

Makin, A. (1998b) 'Foreign Capital, Growth and External Adjustment' *Economia Internazionale*, vol. 60(2), pp. 229–38.

Makin, A. (1999a) 'The Great East Asian Capital Flow Reversal: Reasons, Responses and Ramifications', *The World Economy*, vol. 22(3), pp. 407–19.

Makin, A. (1999b) 'Preventing Financial Crises in East Asia', *Asian Survey*, vol. 39, No. 4, pp. 668–78.

Makin, A. and Robson, A. (1999) 'Comparing Capital and Trade Weighted Measures of Australia's Effective Exchange Rate' *Pacific Economic Review*, vol. 4 (2), pp. 203–14.

Malkiel, B. (1989) 'Efficient Markets Hypothesis', in Eatwell, J., Milgate, M. and Newman, P. (eds), *The New Palgrave: Finance*, Macmillan, London.

Mankiw, N., Romer, D. and Weil, D. (1992) 'A Contribution to the Empirics of Economic Growth', *Quarterly Journal of Economics*, vol. 107, (2), May, pp. 407–37.

Markowitz, H. (1952) 'Portfolio Selection', *Journal of Finance*, vol. 7, pp. 77–91.

Marston, R. (1985) 'Stabilization Policies in Open Economies', in R. Jones and P. Kenen (eds), *Handbook of International Economics*, vol. 2, North-Holland, Amsterdam.

Marston, R.C. (1995) *International Financial Integration*, New York: Cambridge University Press.

McDermott, C. and Westcott, R. (1996) 'Fiscal Reforms That Work', *Economic Issues 4*, International Monetary Fund, Washington, DC.

McKinnon, R. (1979) *Money in International Exchange*, Oxford University Press, Oxford.

McKinnon, R.I. (1969) 'Portfolio Balance and International Payments Adjustment', in R.A. Mundell and A.K. Swoboda (eds), *Monetary Problems of the International Economy*, University of Chicago Press, Chicago, pp. 199–234.

McKinnon, R.I. (1993) 'International Money in Historical Perspective', *Journal of Economic Literature*, vol. 31(1), pp. 1–44.

Meade, J.E. (1951) *The Balance of Payments*, Oxford University Press, London.

Meerschaum, D.M. (1991) *Breaking Financial Boundaries: Global Capital, National Deregulation and Financial Services*, Harvard Business School.

Mishkin, F.S. (1984) 'Are Real Interest Rates Equal Across Countries? An Empirical Investigation of International Parity Conditions', *Journal of Finance*, vol. 39, pp. 1345–57.

Modigliani, F. (1970) 'The Life Cycle Hypothesis of Saving and Intercountry Differences in the Saving Ratio', in W.A. Eltis, M.F.G. Scott and J.N. Wolfe (eds), *Induction, Growth and Trade: Essays in Honour of Sir Roy Harrod*, Clarendon, London, pp. 197–225.

Mun, T. (1664) *England's Treasure by Foreign Trade or the Balance of Our Foreign Trade is the Rule of Our Treasure*, London.

Mundell, R. (1963) 'Capital Mobility and Stabilization Policy Under Fixed and Flexible Exchange Rates', *Canadian Journal of Economics and Political Science*, vol. 29 November, pp. 475–85.

Mundell, R.A. (1968) *International Economics*, Macmillan, New York.

Mussa, M. (1984) 'The Theory of Exchange Rate Determination', in J. Bilson and R. Marston (eds) *Exchange Rate Theory and Practice*, University of Chicago Press, Chicago.

Newman, P., Milgate, M. and Eatwell, J. (1992) *The New Palgrave Dictionary of Money and Finance*, Macmillan, London.

Niehans, J. (1984) *International Monetary Economics*, Philip Allan, Oxford.

Obstfeld, M. (1986) 'Capital Mobility in the World Economy: Theory and Measurement', *Carnegie-Rochester Conference Series on Public Policy*, vol. 24, pp. 55–104.

Obstfeld, M. and Rogoff, K. (1996) *Foundation of International Macroeconomics*, MIT Press, Massachusetts.

Olson, M. and Bailey, M. (1981) 'Positive Time Preference', *Journal of Political Economy*, vol. 80(1), pp. 1–25.

Oppenheimer, P.M. (1974) 'Non-Traded Goods and the Balance of Payments: An Historical Note', *Journal of Economic Literature*, vol. 12(3), pp. 882–8.

Persson, T. and Svensson, L. (1985) 'Current Account Dynamics and the Terms of Trade', *Journal of Political Economy*, vol. 93(1), pp. 43–65.

Pitchford, J.D. (1995) *The Current Account and Foreign Debt*, Routledge, London.

Polak, J. (1957) 'Monetary Analysis of Income Formation and Payments Problems', *IMF Staff Papers*, vol. 6, pp. 1–50.

Prachowny, MF (1984) *Macroeconomic Analysis for Small Open Economies*, Oxford University Press, Oxford.

Rhomberg, R. (1976) 'Indices of Effective Exchange Rates', *IMF Staff Papers*, vol. 23, pp. 88–103.

Ricardo, D. (1817) *On the Principles of Political Economy and Taxation*, Cambridge, Cambridge University Press, 1951.

Robertson, D.H. (1940) *Essays in Monetary Theory*, P.S. King, London.

Robinson, J. (1937) 'The Foreign Exchanges', in J. Robinson (ed.) *Essays in the Theory of Employment*, Blackwell, Oxford.

Rogoff, K. (1996) 'The Purchasing Power Parity Puzzle', *Journal of Economic Literature*, vol. 34(2), pp. 647–68.

Roll, E. (1961) *A History of Economic Thought*, Faber, London.

Roll, R. (1970) *The Behaviour of Interest Rates*, New York: Basic Books.

Romer, P. (1986) 'Increasing Returns and Long Run Growth', *Journal of Political Economy*, vol. 94, pp. 1002–37.

Ruffin, R.J. (1979) 'Growth and the Long-Run Theory of International Capital Movements', *American Economic Review*, vol. 69(5), pp. 833–42.

Ruffin, R.J. (1984) 'International Factor Movements', in P.B. Kenen and R.W. Jones (eds), *Handbook of International Economics*, vol. 1, North-Holland, Amsterdam, ch. 5, pp. 237–88.

Sachs, J. (1982) 'The Current Account in the Macroeconomic Adjustment Process', *Scandinavian Journal of Economics*, vol. 84(2), pp. 147–59.

Salop, J. and Spitaeller, E. (1980) 'Why Does the Current Account Matter?', *IMF Staff Papers*, vol. 27(2), pp. 101–34.

Salter, W.E.G. (1959) 'Internal and External Balance: The Role of Expenditure and Price Effects', *Economic Record*, vol. 35(71), pp. 226–38.

Scarth, W.M. (1988) *Macroeconomics: An Introduction to Advanced Methods*, Harcourt Brace Jovanovich, Toronto.

Seater, J. (1993) 'Ricardian Equivalence', *Journal of Economic Literature*, vol. 31(1), pp. 142–90.

Sinn, S. (1990) *Net External Asset Positions of 145 Countries: Estimation and Interpretation*, Kieler Studien 234, Institut fur Weltwirtschaft an der Universitat, Kiel.

Smith, A. (1776) *An Inquiry into the Nature and Causes of the Wealth of Nations*, New York, Random House, 1937.

Solnik, B. (1991) *International Investments* 2nd ed., Addison Wesley, Reading, Massachusetts.

Solow, R. (1956) 'A Contribution to the Theory of Economic Growth', *Quarterly Journal of Economics*, vol. 70, pp. 65–94.

Stern, R.M. (1972) *The Balance of Payments*, Macmillan, Basingstoke.

Stiglitz, J. (1985) 'Credit Markets and the Control of Capital', *Journal of Money, Credit and Banking*, vol. 17(2), pp. 133–52.

Swan, T. (1955) 'Larger Run Problems of the Balance of Payments', Paper Presented at the Congress of the ANZAAS, Melbourne, published in H.W. Arndt and M.W. Corden (eds), (1963), *The Australian Economy: A Volume of Readings*, Melbourne, Cheshire Press, 384–95; reprinted in R.E. Caves and H. O. Johnson (eds), (1968), *A.E.A. Readings in International Economics*, vol. 11, Richard Irwin, Homewood, Illinois, pp. 455–64.

Swan, T. (1956) 'Economic Growth and Capital Accumulation', *Economic Record*, vol. 32, November, pp. 334–61.

Taylor, M (1995) 'The Economics of Exchange Rates', *Journal of Economic Literature*, vol. 33(1), pp. 13–47.

Throop, A.W. (1994) 'International Financial Market Integration and Linkages of National Interest Rates', *Federal Reserve Bank of San Francisco Economic Review*, vol. 3, pp. 3–18.

Tinbergen, J. (1952) *On the Theory of Economic Policy*, North-Holland, Amsterdam.

Tobin, J. (1958) 'Liquidity Preference as Behaviour Toward Risk', *Review of Economic Studies*, vol. 25(1), pp. 65–86.

Tobin, J. (1969) 'A General Equilibrium Approach to Monetary Theory', *Journal of Money, Credit and Banking*, vol. 1(1), pp. 15–29.

Tobin, J. (1978) 'A Proposal for International Monetary Reform', *Eastern Economic Journal*, vol. 4, pp. 153–9.

Tobin, J. (1984) 'On the Efficiency of the Financial System', *Lloyds Bank Review London*, July, pp. 1–15.

Tsiang, S.C. (1961) 'The Role of Money in Trade-Balance Stability: Synthesis of the Elasticity and Absorption Approaches', *American Economic Review*, vol. 51, pp. 912–36.

Tsiang, S.C. (1989) 'Loanable Funds', in J. Eatwell, M. Milgate and P. Newman (eds), *The New Palgrave: Money*, London: Macmillan, pp. 190–4.

United Nations (1949) *International Capital Movements During the Inter-War Period*, United Nations, New York.

United Nations (1993) *System of National Accounts*, United Nations, New York.

United Nations, *United Nations Monthly Bulletin of Statistics*, various issues, United Nations, New York.

Van der Ploeg, F. (1994) *The Handbook of International Macroeconomics*, Blackwell, Oxford.

Webb, L.R. (1970) 'The Role of International Capital Movements in Trade and Growth', in I. McDougall and R. Snape (eds) *Studies in International Economics*, North-Holland, Amsterdam, ch. 13, pp. 225–66.

Williamson, J. (1996) 'Globalisation, Convergence and History', *Journal of Economic History*, vol. 56, June, pp. 277–306.

World Bank (1993) *The East Asian Miracle – Economic Growth and Public Policy*, Oxford University Press, Oxford.

World Bank (1998) *Private Capital Flows to Developing Countries: The Road to Financial Integration*, World Bank Policy Research Report.

Index